Jatakamāla

or

A Garland of Birth Stories

Boro-Budhur Temple

Jatakamāla

or

A Garland of Birth Stories

by

Marie Musæus – Higgins

Low Price Publications

Delhi-110052

Distributed By
D K Publishers Distributors P Ltd.
24, Ansari Road, Darya Ganj,
New Delhi-110002
Phones: 51562573-77
Fax : 51562578
visit us at: www.dkpd.com
e-mail: dkpd@del3.vsnl.net.in

First Published 1914

Reprinted in **LPP** 2005

ISBN 81-7536-383-5

Published by
Low Price Publications
A-6, Nimri Commercial Centre,
Near Ashok Vihar Phase-IV,
Delhi-110052
Phone: 27452453
visit us at: www.lppindia.com
e-mail: lpp@nde.vsnl.net.in

Printed at
D K Fine Art Press P Ltd.
Delhi-110052

PRINTED IN INDIA

JATAKAMÂLA

OR

A GARLAND OF BIRTH STORIES

BY

MARIE MUSÆUS—HIGGINS

Author of "Stories from the History of Ceylon"

COLOMBO:

Printed at the Boys' Industrial Home Press, Wellawatte

1914

Dedicated

TO

ALL MY CHILDREN.

CONTENTS

PART II.

LIST OF ILLUSTRATIONS.

Bird's-eye view of Bora-budhur Temple.

FOREWORD

This is a necklace of pearls, and the string is the One Life that runs as a golden thread through all; and the pearls are each one a life of the Exalted One, the Brother of man, the Bodhisattva. As He passes along our path of involution and evolution, He is a symbol of man's life, progressing or falling back again, gathering divers experience until He needs no further births. And what is this unknown Force thus symbolised? In the mineral it sleeps and stirs not, in the plant it dreams and feebly moves, and in the animal it wakes and gains the senses one by one, till in the man the spark becomes a flame, and at last the Man is more than man. "Beings arise," said the Buddha, "from previous happenings. Tanhā, desire of existence, is the cause. Rise and fall is the natural law. But this round of birth and death may end. Cut off desire of life and be born no more!"

We are not left without a Teacher. There are always Masters in the world, some steps in advance of the common herd of men; and it must be so in the lower grades of life as well. Thus, the elephant is the sage of animals, the lion is the king of beasts of prey, the whale the mammoth of the sea, and the eagle rules the haunters of the sky. Embodied in turn as each of these, and then again as man, the Teacher of gods and men performs His work. So also tell the Purānas ; they speak of the One Life as tortoise, as fish, as boar, as half-man, as warrior, as sage. And so tell these ancient tales, recalling times, as we learnt at our nurses' knee, "when animals had power of speech, in the good old times, when Brahmadatta ruled at Benares, long long ago." Thus moral teachings are put in the mouth of an animal, to show that they too have a share in our evolution, and there are lessons that we men can learn from animals ; wisdom from the elephant, devotion from the dog, caution from the tortoise, fickleness of mind from the monkey and how to avoid all that, and so through many tales. In this unity of life our fates are linked with theirs. We rise and lift them too ; they too in the lapse of ages will be men like us. When the poor shell can no longer hold the mighty power within, it bursts, and He is released and is an embodied thing no more.

The sacrifice of the Bodhisattva is that He willingly limits Himself, and stays to turn the wheel of life that men may not be utterly disheartened by the task. And so when He had found and conquered He sang triumphantly :—

Aneka jātisaṃsāram sandhāvissam anibbisam
Gahakāram gavesanto, dukkhā jāti punappunam.
Gahakāraka diṭṭho 'si, puna geham na kāhasi,
Sabbā te phāsukā bhaggā, gahakuṭam visaṃkhitam.

Thro' many a round of birth and death I ran,
Nor found the builder that I sought. Life's stream
Is birth and death and birth, with sorrow filled.
Now, house builder, thou'rt seen ! No more shalt build !
Broken are all thy rafters, split thy beam !

F. L. WOODWARD.

Mahinda College, Galle,
27th March, 1914.

One of the entrances to Galleries at the Boro-Budhur Temple

INTRODUCTION.

Wesak Day[1] of the year 2455 of the Buddhist Era had dawned over the Island of Ceylon. The Sinhalese Buddhists were rejoicing. They were preparing early in the morning to go to the Temples with their flower offerings to be laid at the feet of the Statues of the Lord Buddha, in memory of Him, who taught the Dhamma. The temples were adorned with flags and graceful arches of young coconut leaves.

Women and men clad in white, thus marking their vow of taking Attha-Sila[2] and carrying on their heads flat baskets, filled with sweet smelling white and yellow flowers, walked in procession to the nearest temples. Here, small heaps of flowers, laid before the statues, indicated that other devout Buddhists had already preceded them in their devotion to their religion and to the memory of their Lord.

The greatest crowds of Buddhists had gathered in the old city of Anuradhapura, where more than two thousand years ago, Buddhism had been introduced into Lanka by Mahinda[3], the son of the Indian Buddhist Emperor Asoka. Mahinda had preached the first sermon on Buddhism to the Sinhalese King Devānampiya-Tissa, who reigned at that time in Lanka. King Tissa had been so much impressed with what he heard that he dedicated his kingdom to Buddhism, taking the shafts of the golden State plough[4] in his own hands he drew a circle with it round Anurādhapura. Mahinda had given his blessing and from that time Buddhism had begun to spread rapidly over the Island.

At the present day, Buddhists gather again from all parts of the Island and place flowers before the temple ruins of the old city of Anurādhapura.

On this special Fullmoon-Day of Wesak, 2455 A. B., thousands of devoted Buddhists had come to Anurādhapura and from early morning they made pilgrimages to the Isurumuniya-Temple [5] the Ruanweli-Dagaba [6] and the Holy Bodhi-Tree, [7] the oldest historical tree in the world, still standing and preaching as it were to the young generation, of the glories of ancient Buddhist Lanka.

All these white-clad people look so solemn and feel so happy and move around so quietly and so orderly. Surely they must still be full of devotion to their ancient faith!

Such are the sights seen on Wesak-Day all over Buddhist Ceylon.

"And how are we to celebrate Wesak-Day, children?" said the white mother to her dark-eyed maidens, who had gathered round to give her the greetings of the Day.

"Oh, mother dear" said Leelawatti, "let us first go to the Temple together and offer flowers and then please tell one of the stories of the Buddha's former births, which you promised you would tell us. We are only a few girls here just now in the holidays and we ought to have some reward for staying here, instead of going home like the other girls."

"Yes, little one" answered the mother. "I too think that this day is the best day for making a beginning to tell the Buddha's Birth-stories. So after we return from the Temple, let us sit down in the Bamboo-grove in our garden, near our little Shrine-Room and then we will commence our garland of Birth-stories."

The sun was just sinking behind the coconut palms, flooding the garden with its red and golden hues when the little group of Sinhalese girls gathered round their white mother in the bamboo-grove eager to hear the story which she had promised to tell.

And the mother said: "Children, my stories this time, are of a different kind from the former ones. They are not all like the Stories from the History of Ceylon,[8] they are tales of the former births of the Lord Buddha, when he was a Bodhisattva, when he was still on the road to Perfection, to Buddhahood.

They are called 'Jâtakamālâ, or a Garland of Birth-stories,' because, the original writer of these Stories said that: He would devoutly worship the 'wonderful exploits which the Muni performed in previous births, by a poem, the verses of which would be like the flowers in a garland.'

My stories are from the *Sanskrit*, not from the *Pāli*. And the old Scribe of these Jâtaka-mālâ writes about them thus: 'They teach the way leading to Buddhahood. They are the landmarks of that Path. Even the hard-hearted may be softened by them. For the benefit of mankind these stories are written and they are in accordance with the course of facts as recorded by Scripture Tradition.'

The pictures to the stories are from a very famous Temple in Jāva, the Boro-Budhur Temple ([9]), which was re-discovered from under the earth and jungle, about sixty years ago, and on its terraces many Jātaka-stories are illustrated by carvings on rock.

But, children, before I begin my Jâtaka-mālâ, I would like you to understand fully, what is meant by a "Buddha" and I will quote from Col. H. S. Olcott's well-known Buddhist Catechism the following explanation of that word. 'A Buddha is not a God, but He is the wisest, noblest and most holy being, who has developed Himself in the course of countless births far beyond all other beings.'

The One, who has resolved to become a Buddha, strives in each of His births to become better and wiser, till at last He becomes perfect, He becomes illuminated, He becomes a Buddha; for "Buddha" means the "Perfect," the "All-Wise" the "Enlightened."

Before He reaches this high state of perfection, He is called "Bodhisattva," that means, as I have just told you: "He, who is on the "Road to Perfection." And so in all these stories, the future Buddha will be called "Bodhisattva," till He reaches Buddhahood in His last earthlife, as Prince Siddhartha, the son of King Suddhodana and Queen Māha-Māya of Kapilavastu in India."

The Jatakamālâ has been translated from the original Sanskrit by Professor J. S. Speyer, Dr. Phl., of Leyden, who published them in English in a Dutch Magazine, which was kindly lent me by another Dutch Professor of Batavia, Jāva. Dr. Speyer has very kindly allowed me to use his translation in my own way and to make it popular, which I hope to accomplish. The matter for the last story of the Jâtakamālâ is not from Prof. Speyer's translation. I consulted Edwin Arnold's "Light of Asia," Dr. Paul Carus' "Gospel of Buddha" and Dr. Pleyte's German translation of the "Lalitavishtara," so as to give, if possible, a more complete account of the life story of Prince Siddhartha, the last life on earth of the Bodhisattva.

The illustrations to the Jâtakas are from Photographs of the carvings of the Boro-Budhur Temple in Jāva. The photos were kindly sent me by Major van Erp, who had been deputed by the Dutch Government to restore this Temple. He gave me permission to use them in illustrating this little book.

M. MUSÆUS HIGGINS.

The. Hare and his three friends.

JATAKA STORIES

I.

THE STORY OF THE HARE

There is a beautiful story told about the Bodhisattva when, as it is said, he was born on earth in the shape of a hare. The story runs thus :—

There once lived in a forest in India, which was often visited by ascetics and wise people, a very clever hare. This forest was a magnificent place, where flowers, fruits and lovely creepers grew plentifully and where a river, with its deep blue waters, rolled down gently murmuring into the valley.

The Bodhisattva, in the form of the hare, lived near this river with three friends, an otter, a monkey and a jackal.

The hare was considered by his friends almost like a king, as they believed that he was superior to any other animal. He was a teacher to his friends as well as to the other smaller animals, and he lived the life of an ascetic. Even the bigger animals respected him, and they did not harm him, but listened to his teachings like pupils and friends.

So he lived with his three friends in harmony and peace, and his virtuous life and the practice of compassion for others was so great that his reputation reached even the world of the Devas.

One evening, the three friends came to the hare to hear him preach the Law to them. They were reverentially sitting at his feet. The moon showed herself half hidden by the branches of the trees and looked like a bright round mirror. When the Bodhisattva (the hare) saw the moon he said to his companions: "See! the moon with its face almost full smilingly reminds us that to-morrow will be full-moon day, the greatest of the Poya-days. So to-morrow, we must perform the duties which are prescribed for Poya-days.* We must not satisfy our own body with food, till we have honoured some guest, who chances to come in our way, with some good food, obtained in a right way—which means without destroying life.

Life is short as a flash of lightning, therefore guard against destroying life. You must gain further merit by charitable deeds which have good conduct for their key-note. Merit is the source of happiness, therefore be ready to seize every opportunity of practising it. Leave the path of demerit, for misfortune and dishonour are underlying it."

---

* Poya-days are the religious festival days of the Buddhists. They are the days of new moon, full-moon and first and last quarter-moon.

After the Great One, in the shape of a hare, had given these teachings to his friends, they left him, bowing reverently to him. Then the Bodhisattva became very thoughtful and said to himself: "My friends are able to give suitable food to a guest who may happen to come here on the morrow; but what can I do for him, the honoured guest, to whom I have nothing to give. "The blades of grass which make my food would not be suitable for any guest whether human or animal. Oh! what is the use of my life, when I am not able to feed any stranger properly? This is a great grief to me!"

"But, why should I grieve? Have I not my own body, which belongs to me, which is my property and belongs to nobody else? I know now how I can honour the expected guest when he comes and how I can give him the best I have. With this miserable body of mine I will practise hospitality."

After these thoughts the hare went back to his home, joyfully waiting for the guest, who might be expected next day.

But the Devas had heard this vow and the Earth began to shake with joy, and flowers showered over the Great One, and the wind blew the sweet-smelling flower-dust towards him and the clouds took a beautiful rosy colour and smiled on him.

The Devas in Devaloka rejoiced and the king of the Devas, Sakra,* made up his mind to test the hare and see whether he would sacrifice his body for the benefit of a hungry guest.

So, the following day, at noon, when the sun throws out its hottest rays and when the sky is filled with so much radiant light, that it cannot be looked at; when in the jungle the insects hum the loudest; when the birds hide themselves in the branches of the trees to find a cool resting place and when the strength of the traveller is exhausted with heat and fatigue, then Sakra in the garb of a Brahman mendicant came down as it seemed half dead of hunger and heat, and sat under a tree not far from the place where the hare and his three friends were living.

He groaned pitifully and said: "Here I am alone and lost in the jungle far from my friends, Oh! ye pious ones, help me, for I am dying of hunger and fatigue. Who will give me hospitality in my great need?"

The four friends, who had been looking out for a hungry guest, heard the prayer of the Brahman and quickly they ran to the tree under which he was resting.

They beheld the tired traveller and said to him: "Welcome, Oh! beloved one! Do not be sad and troubled any more, for with us you are

---

* Sakra, the king of the Devas, has a rock throne on which he sits. When any deserving person on earth needs help his throne gets hot. He looks down to earth and he generally helps the person in need. When anybody does a great deed on earth his rock throne begins to shake.

as with your own disciples. Grant us the favour of accepting our hospitality to-day; to-morrow you may go on wherever you wish."

The Brahman silently consented, and the otter with a joyful heart ran to his lair and brought seven rohita-fishes, which he offered to the hungry Brahman and said: "These seven fishes I found on dry ground, I did not take them out of the water and so you can accept them without doubt on this blessed full-moon day. They might have been forgotten by a fisherman or have jumped out of the water themselves. Take them and satisfy your hunger which almost kills you and then rest."

Then the jackal appeared with one lizard and a bowl of sour-milk, which must have been left by a traveller, as he had found it on the road side, not far away. Bowing low before the Brahman he offered his gifts and asked him to eat them and rest.

Then the monkey came and said: "Ripe mangoes, cool water, refreshing shade, I offer you, reverend Brahman. Enjoy these gifts and stay with us this night."

Then the hare approached reverently, bowed down before the Brahman and said: "A hare, who has grown up in the forest has neither rice nor beans to offer, so accept my body as the gift of hospitality from me. Cooked on a fire my body will be acceptable. Feed on it and stay here for the night in this hermitage."

Sakra (in the shape of the Brahman) who was wondering whether the hare really meant to offer his own body, answered: "How could I kill you, a living being, who has showed friendship to me. No! no! go in peace, I cannot accept your offer."

The hare replied: "Your answer shows me that you are full of compassion, which suits well your office as a teacher. You must at least allow me to rest here and I will think how I can show you my hospitality."

Sakra, the King of Devas, could understand the thoughts of the hare, who was really trying to find out how he could offer his body as a gift of hospitality to the Brahman. So he let the hare rest, while he was preparing his food, which had been given him by the otter, the jackal, and the monkey.

Now Sakra made a fire of charcoal, blazing on the ground without smoke and leaping up in golden flames. The hare looked at this fire with gladness and bowing again before the Brahman said: "It is my duty to be charitable and I have found in you a worthy guest. I must not neglect this opportunity for hospitality, so I implore you to accept this boon from me, oh! Brahman, which is given to you with joy."

With these words the hare threw himself into the blazing fire, like the immortal Hamsa plunging into a pool of smiling lotuses.

The flames did not give the hare any pain, but closed round his body like a golden cloud!

And Sakra, the King of the Devas, in admiration and reverence, re-assuming his own shining form took the body of the hare reverently out of the flames and lifting it up aloft exclaimed: "Behold, ye Devas, inhabitants of the celestial worlds; behold and rejoice at this astonishing deed of this Great Being! He sacrificed his body to me as food to his guest, though he did not know who I was. He had nothing else to give and so he gave himself! What a difference between him and the species to which he belonged! He puts to shame the gods as well as men with his charity."

In order to make this deed known to the Devas as well as to mankind, Sakra put an emblem of the hare in his own palace and in the hall of the Devas and from that night, the full-moon night, the form of the hare is seen in the moon, where like an image reflected in a silver mirror, on full-moon nights, it preaches to mankind the virtue of charity.

And the three friends of the hare—the otter, the jackal, and the monkey—disappeared from earth and were welcomed in the Deva-world as the friends of the Great One, who had sacrificed his body in charity for a hungry Brahman.

II.

THE STORY OF THE WONDERFUL FISH.

The following story illustrates the "Power of Truth."

It is said that once the Bodhisattva çame to earth as the chief of the fish, in a small but beautiful lake. This lake was covered with white, pink, and blue lotus, and on its deep blue waters, swans, ducks and geese sported in glee. The borders of the lake were embellished with flowering trees and shrubs, which showered their red and yellow blossoms on the water, so that the lake seemed covered with garlands of flowers.

The Bodhisattva, even when taking the form of a fish, remembered the practice of good deeds, which he learned in some of his former incarnations, and he tried to teach the fish of his own shoal, as though they were his children He taught them to be kind to each other, and never to injure one smaller or weaker, than themselves, and so the fish under his rule became prosperous and led better lives than others of their kind.

One hot season the Rain-God, Parjanya by name, being angry with the creatures of the earth, prevented the rain from falling. The fierce rays of the sun drank up a great deal of the water from the lake.

Before the rain.

The earth also was so thirsty with fever, that she quenched her thirst at the lake.

The wind too, being heated by the fierce sun rays, rushed to the lake for refreshment, and so the water in the lake became less and less, and it looked more like a pond than a lake, and the poor fish had hardly enough water to cover their bodies.

To add to their distress, caused by the scarcity of water, crowds of birds gathered round the diminishing lake, ready to pounce upon the fish, should they show themselves on the surface. The chief of the fish felt the great distress of his shoal, which seemed doomed to perish, either by want of water, or by being devoured by the hungry crows or other birds watching their opportunity. The surface of the lake was daily diminishing, and, if no rain came soon there would be no help for them all. There was no chance for them to find another lake or river either, for their enemies were everywhere watching to pounce upon them.

The Bodhisattva meditated, and turning to the sky, with a deep sigh, he said: "As it is true that I do not recollect ever having done the slightest harm to any living being, even in my worst distress, by the power of this truth, may the Lord of the Devas fill this lake with the water of his rains."

So strong was this appeal, and so irresistible the power of Truth, that a miracle straightway occurred. The God of Rain, Parjanya, chased all the rain-clouds before him, and soon the sky was filled with heavy black clouds. Lightnings, like merry dancers, played amongst the gloomy clouds, and thunder claps re-echoed as music to these dances.

Then like a shower of pearls the raindrops fell. The peacocks spreading out their tails like fans, danced gaily round the lake in their joy, screaming with delight. The thirsty earth, drinking up the fruitful rain, sent out a sweet scent of satisfaction from her surface, and the mountains poured their gurgling streams into the valleys, and the lake began slowly to fill, bringing hope of life back to the half-dead fish.

The crows and other birds had fled as soon as the thunderstorm began. But the chief of the fishes, though full of gratitude and happiness, wished it to rain on for a long time, and he turned to the Rain-God, Parjanya and said: "Roar Parjanya, roar! a roaring loud and deep, depriving the crows of their joy, pouring out thy water-treasure like jewels of lustrous brilliancy."

When Sakra, the King of the Devas heard this, he came in person to the Bodhisattva (the chief of the fishes) and said: "Without doubt, it is thy truthfulness, Lord of the fishes, which has induced Parjanya to pour out the rain-water from the clouds, as water flows from an overturned water-pot. I feel guilty in not having attended more to Thy wants, who thinkest only of the wants of others. Therefore be no longer anxious as to the water supply of Thy lake. The region where Thy virtue reigns shall never be visited by a similar drought."

After the rain.

After saying this, Sakra disappeared.

The lake became large in expanse, and joyously the fishes sported about in it, and never again, so long as the Lord of the fishes lived in this lake, did a like calamity occur.

III.

THE STORY OF THE BIRD WHICH COULD NOT BE BURNT.

Once upon a time, when the Bodhisattva had not yet reached human birth, he was born in a bird's nest as a quail.

He had many brothers and sisters, who grew rapidly as they were fed by worms and every kind of coarse food which their parents could find. But the Bodhisattva remembering the commandment that no living being should be killed, would not eat anything but seeds, figs and such vegetable food as was put before the young birds by their parents.

So he did not grow fast as the other young birds, but his body was much more delicate and more refined than theirs. But when his brothers and sisters could already use their wings and fly about he had to stay in the nest and watch them amusing themselves.

One day, a forest-fire broke out, not far from where the young quails dwelt. They heard a great noise. They saw clouds of smoke and at last some sparks flying about. The wind rose and fanned the flames into a whirling motion, as if figures with arms and limbs of flame, shaking their smoke-hair, were performing wild dances.

The animals and birds of the forest fled in terror and the flames, as if in pursuit of them, swept over the trembling grasses and bushes, covering them with their fiery tongues and burning them to ashes.

Further and further spread the fire until it came to the bush where the quail's nest was. The air was quivering from the heat and the smoke seemed to suffocate all life around.

With shrieks of fear, the young quails lifted themselves on their small wings and not caring for their weak brother, they flew off, leaving him alone amidst the burning bushes.

But the Bodhisattva was not afraid, as he knew his power, the great power of Truth, which had preserved him in former births also; and when the fire reached up to the nest in which he sat as a poor, forlorn little bird, he spoke to the raging fire gently: "I am not strong and big enough to run or fly away, and my parents and brothers have fled from fear of you. Agni, God of Fire, there is no gift here worth offering to you therefore I ask you in the name of Truth, for which I have lived and now live, to turn back."

When Agni heard these gentle words, uttered by the Bodhisattva, in the shape of a small bird, the fire, although fanned by the wind and finding food in the dry leaves on the ground under the bushes, suddenly stopped as if stemmed by a swollen river.

And the quail and all the birds and animals, which had fled to the bush on which was the nest, were not burnt

Thus the small bird, who through the power of Truth could not be burnt to death or swallowed up by fire, saved that part of the forest in which he lived from the violent attacks of Agni, the Fire-God, who, obedient to the voice of Truth, had put out the fire at once.

It is said that ever since then, up to this day, when there is a forest fire in the Himalaya Mountains, the fire cannot go beyond this famous place, where it stops at once as if charmed by the spell of a many-headed serpent.

So the power of Truth overcame the Fire!

IV.

THE STORY OF THE BUFFALO.

Once the Bodhisattva was born in a big forest in India as a wild buffalo-bull. Why he had to undergo this punishment we do not know, but there must have been some evil Karma for him to work out, and so we find Him, the Great One, descended to the animal state as a buffalo.

The Law of Karma is the law of "Cause and Effect," or the Law of "Justice." "What you sow you reap," and so somehow the Bodhisattva must have deserved some portion of evil Karma, in an incarnation of this kind, in order to learn forbearance or to enable him to practise it, which he did in a great degree during this incarnation as a buffalo-bull.

It is said this buffalo had a very grim appearance. He was covered with mud and the dark-blue grey colour of his skin made him look like a dark, moving rock.

But although in this low animal state, in which generally stupidity is most prevalent, this buffalo was of a very different order. He was gentle and compassionate and had not forgotten, from former lives, the law of righteousness. His natural goodness became known to all animals, but some wicked animals took advantage of it and played tricks on him and tried to vex him in order t see how far his forbearance would go.

Now a wicked-minded monkey who wanted to find out whether anger or wrath had power over him, always put himself in the way of the buffalo.

When he was hungry and grazing peacefully, the monkey would throw himself right before him, and when he good-naturedly turned round to go to another spot, the monkey was again before him, glaring at him and grinning in a disagreeable manner, as if he wanted

The Buffalo and the Monkey.

to say : " I am not afraid of you, you ugly old buffalo'" When the buffalo was asleep, resting contentedly among the bushes, the monkey would suddenly spring on his head and jump between his horns, or he would dance on his back. Sometimes the monkey would take a stick and prick his ears with it.

But the most mischievous trick of all happened when the buffalo, who loved the water very much, wanted to take a bath. The monkey jumped at once on his head and put his hands over his eyes so that he could not enjoy his bath, not being able to see where he was going. Sometimes the monkey jumped on his back, took a stick in his hands and used the buffalo as his horse.

He imitated Death this way, as in old Hindu temples Yama, Death is represented as riding a buffalo.

In this way the poor buflalo was tormented day by day ; but he never lost his patience and he thought that this was a good lesson for him. These trials of patience went so far that a yaksha, seeing one day the monkey using the buffalo as his horse, put himself before the buffalo and said : "Why are you so patient ? Why do you become the slave of this impudent monkey ? Do you not know your own strength ? You could teach him a good lesson, which he would never forget. You are as strong as a lion, and by the trampling of your feet, or by using your horns, you could kill a lion I have never seen a monkey cured of his impudence by gentleness and forbearance." The buffalo answered mildly: "Surely I know my strength and I would not use it upon this silly little monkey, who has no power of defending himself against me. If he were as strong as I am or stronger than I, then I would not use forbearance toward him."

"Ill treatment received from a powerless animal gives the best opportunity for practising virtue, and forbearance can only be taught us by another. So as this feeble, fickle monkey is teaching me forbearance, therefore why should I get angry?"

Then the yaksha said: "Then you will never get rid of these vexations! Who shall punish this rascal, if you do not put your humble forbearance aside?"

The buffalo answered: "I am longing for happiness and content and I do not want to hurt anybody. Besides, I am trying to teach him and to wake his conscience. If he does not learn and does not understand my teaching, he will some day meet some one with a hasty temper. Then he will get his punishment for his naughty doings and I shall get rid of his disagreeable tricks."

The yaksha was quite amazed hearing these kind words of the tormented buffalo and called out: "How wonderful that a buffalo should possess such a degree of forbearance and patience. You must be a great being, and have assumed this animal shape for some purpose. Surely you have taught me a lesson which I shall not forget."

The Buffalo and the Yak ha.

After these words the yaksha threw the insolent monkey off the back of the patient buffalo and bade him, under the threat of severe punishment, leave the buffalo in peace.

An excellent object lesson in Patience and Forbearance.

V.

THE STORY OF THE WOODPECKER

The Bodhisattva was once upon a time born as a woodpecker.

This woodpecker was different from all other birds. He was not only wise but also specially beautiful. His feathers shone with a splendid gloss of different colours, and, when he spread out his wings, he flew with such stateliness, that he was acknowledged in the forest, where he lived, as the king of birds.

His food, because of the species to which he belonged at that time, consisted of worms which had to be extracted from the trunks of trees. All woodpeckers peck at the trunks of trees in order to find out whether they are hollow. In the jungle you can hear many of them at work. When a part of a tree sounds hollow, they pick out the grubs and eat them. But this woodpecker was very different from his kind. He did not want to injure any living creature, not even a worm, and so he lived on the young shoots of the branches of trees, on fruits and flowers.

He had not forgotten the five Precepts, and, when the occasion came, he used to gather birds and animals round him and preach to them about the law of righteousness.

He was also like a wise physician, who helped his fellow-creatures when they were in distress, and he did not expect even thanks for the trouble he took. So the woodpecker lived in happiness and contentment in his forest and all the animals and birds around him were happy and contented too.

With the intention of helping any creature in distress, our woodpecker was flitting about the forests one day, when he saw a lion, who was certainly either very ill or in great pain. He was writhing on the ground with his mane all tangled, and he was groaning in a very painful way. "What ails you, king of the animals?" called out the woodpecker. "Have you been struck by a poisonous arrow, or are you ill, or have you been fighting with elephants or have you been indulging in too much meat? Tell me what is the matter with you, for perhaps I can help you."

The lion answered: "Skilful king of the birds, I am not ill, nor have I indulged in too much fighting, but a bone sticks in my throat, which gives me as much pain as though it were an arrow. I can neither swallow it nor can I

The woodpecker flew into the open jaws of the lion.

get it out. If you can help me, you will do a good work." "I can help you," answered the woodpecker after thinking for a little while. "Just follow my directions and I will pull this bone out of your throat and ease you of your pain."

Then the woodpecker picked up a piece of strong wood, told the lion to open his mouth as wide as he could, and put the wood into his mouth, in order to keep the mouth open without giving the lion a chance of closing it Then the woodpecker flew into the open jaws of the lion and with great skill loosened the bone first at one end and then at the other, pulling it successfully out of the lion's throat.

Then he removed the piece of wood from the lion's mouth and stood before him with glad eyes, being very contented that he had delivered him from great pain and from certain death by suffocation or starvation.

The lion was very glad to be relieved of his pain but he thought it was a great honour for the woodpecker to have been permitted to act as surgeon to him. He murmured a short word of thanks and stalked away to his den to sleep off the exertion of having his mouth prised open and the pain of the bone in his throat, thinking very little of the great service done him by the woodpecker.

The woodpecker flew off, very happy that on this day he had saved the life of a fellow creature.

One day some time later, the woodpecker was searching in vain for food. A drought had scorched the young shoots of the trees and the fruits were also dried up. He was almost dead of hunger. Then he saw, while he was slowly flying about, the same lion, whom he had saved, feasting on a freshly killed antelope. He was enjoying himself to such a degree, that he did not seem to see anything else.

So the woodpecker came down, stood modestly near the lion, without saying anything and just looked at him with hungry eyes. The lion did not pay any attention to the bird and pretended not to see him.

"He does not recognise me," thought the woodpecker, and he drew quite near and very humbly said: "I come to you to-day like a mendicant, asking you for a little food, as I am starving. You will acquire much merit, if you will help a starving creature."

But the lion growled and said: "I need my food for myself. How dare you come near me? Are you tired of life and do you wish to see the other world? Is it not enough that I allowed you to get out of my jaws once. I have no unmanly mercy?" And he continued his meal, casting a threatening glance at the hungry woodpecker.

Without saying a single word the woodpecker flew upwards, showing the lion that as he was a bird he could not harm him.

When one of the forest Deva's saw this, he became very indignant at the ingratitude

The lion was feasting on an antilope

and greediness of the lion, and he asked the woodpecker: "Why do you not punish this ungrateful animal, as you have the power to do? You are his benefactor and he has treated you with ingratitude and cruelty! Why do you not fly down and peck his eyes out as a punishment for his ingratitude? You can even take some of his meal away from him, being a bird! Why do you stand this ill-treatment?"

"Do not speak thus" answered the woodpecker. "It is not my business to punish an ill-doer, he will get his punishment without my interference, for who will in future help him, when he is in need? I do not regret having done good to him, for I have gained merit by it for the future life. If I had done it to him in order to get something for it in return, it would have been a loan only, not a deed of mercy. If I returned evil for evil I should only destroy my good reputation. It seems to me that the following teaching suits this case:—

"He whose heart is not touched by a service done by a virtuous person is to be left alone gently, but without harshness or anger!"

The Deva wondered at the sayings of the woodpecker and bowing low before him exclaimed: "You surely must be a Rishi, or a Muni, for you have the virtues of a great teacher. I see that not even the form of a bird, which you wear, can hide your wisdom."

And then, honouring him as he would a Brahman, he disappeared.

But the woodpecker flew away sad at the ingratitude of the lion, but with no wrath in his heart.

This story teaches that, even if treated ungratefully, we should practise forbearance towards our enemies, as did the woodpecker to the ungrateful lion.

VI.

THE STORY OF THE KURU-DEER

The following story teaches how the virtuous often suffer more from the pains of others than from their own.

Once the Bodhisattva lived as a Kuru-Deer in a wild forest where splendid trees and bushes grew and where all kinds of animals, large and small had their abode.

His body was very beautiful. His skin shone like gold and the spots on it like jewels of different kinds. But, as he knew the cruelty of man and that his beautiful body would surely attract the eyes of hunters, he withdrew deep into the forest, far away from the habitations of people. He also warned those animals which followed him to avoid snares, traps and nets laid down by hunters to trap them. The animals looked upon him as a teacher.

One day the Bodhisattva (in the shape of the deer) heard a cry of distress coming from the river, which was very swift and full at that time, being swollen by recent rains. He ran quickly to it and saw a man clinging to the branch of a tree and being swiftly carried away down stream. He seemed almost exhausted.

The deer heard him calling out: "Oh, help me, help me, for I am almost exhausted and I can't get out!"

The Bodhisattva, who felt the pains of others more than his own and who had saved very many lives in his re-births in the world called out in a human voice: "Do not fear, I will help you!"

Then, like a brave warrior, not thinking of his own danger, he jumped into the stream and put himself just in front of the exhausted man and called to him to climb on his back. The man managed to follow the directions, and so the deer carried him half-dead out of the river with great exertion.

When the deer had put the man down on the grass he warmed him with his own warm body and, after he had regained his strength, showed him the way back to his village.

The rescued man said: "No friend or relative has done for me as much as thou hast My life therefore ought to be thine. What can I do to show thee my gratitude?" The Bodhisattva answered: "Gratitude is expected from a gentleman, but it is not always shown. Though it ought to come naturally, it is now called a '**virtue**' if it is practised.

Practise this virtue yourself by not telling any human being about my rescuing you. My beautiful body, shining with its brilliant skin, would be an easy prey to covetous hunters, and therefore where I am ought not to be known. This is the only favour I ask from you. I speak honestly to you, being an animal not knowing deceit. Men might in their great convetousness come to kill me, if you praise my beauty and my strength. So guard your tongue and do not speak about me."

The man promised to be silent about the beautiful Kuru-Deer and went home full of gratitude.

In the capital of the kingdom to which the forest belonged and in which the Kuru-Deer lived, there was a king, whose favourite queen was a beautiful and accomplished woman. She often had prophetic dreams and the king generally tried to have these dreams interpreted.

So one night this queen dreamt that she saw a beautiful Kuru-Deer with a golden skin sitting on a throne and preaching the Law in a human voice to the King and Queen and a great many people.

The Queen awoke after this dream just when the morning drums* sounded the morning-call for the king to awake from his night's slumber. She at once went to him and told him her dream and expressed a great wish to possess this jewel-Deer.

---

* The Kings in olden times used to he awakened every morning by the sound of drums.

The king, knowing that the queen's dreams generally came to pass, ordered that all his hunters should try to find it. Besides he had proclaimed by beat of drums that anybody who could give information regarding a beautiful golden deer, whose skin looked as if covered with jewels, should receive a handsome reward.

Now the man who had been rescued by the Kuru-Deer was very poor, and, when he heard the proclamation of the king, he forgot his promise to the deer that he should not tell anybody about its existence, and he went to the king and told him that he had seen such a splendid deer and that he knew where to find it.

The king was delighted and ordered the man to show this precious deer to him.

So he went with the man, accompanied by a few chosen attendants, and had his retinue enclose the place where the deer was to be found. The king was ready to shoot the deer himself and the man conducted him to the place where the Kuru-Deer was staying.

When the man caught sight of the unsuspecting deer, he raised his arm and, pointing to the deer called out: "There he is, your Majesty. Look at him."

To the terror of the ungrateful man, as soon as he pointed to the deer, his hand fell off his arm, as if cut off by a sword. That was the punishment for his treachery. The king, intent on obtaining the deer which he perceived among the dark bushes shining like the moon behind the clouds, strung, his bow and drew cautiously nearer.

The Kuru- Deer, perceiving that he was surrounded by people, saw that he could not run away and so he looked up and said to the king in a human voice : " Pause a moment, O mighty king : do not hit me ; but tell me who was informed you of my existence far away from the dwellings of man ?" The king, astonished at being addressed thus, took still more interest in the beautiful creature before him, and putting down his bow pointed to the ungrateful man and said : " This man has showed me the way to this thicket "

The Bodhisattva at once recognised the man, whom he had rescued and he said : " Shame upon him ! Surely it is true that it is better to save a log of wood from the water than an ungrateful man. I wonder that he did not know that bad Karma would follow him for his ingratitude."

The king became curious as to what all this meant, and he asked the Bodhisattva to ex plain the words he had uttered. So He answered : " I spoke sharp words, because I did not want this man to do such a deed again For, rescuing him from the stream, whose current was carrying him away to the waterfall, I made him promise not to betray my existence to anybody. Now through greed he has forgotten his promise and brought me trouble."

The king cast a piercing glance at the miser-

The Kuru-Deer teaches the Law.

able man, who had already been punished severely by losing his hand, and said: "A man who can be so vile as to betray his rescuer should not live." He bent his bow in order to shoot him. But the Bodhisattva, full of compassion, placed himself between the king and the man and called out: "Stay! your Majesty, stay! Do not kill a man already punished. I stand here to plead for him, for I know how hard his punishment is."

The king, full of admiration, bowed down to the deer and said: "Truly, Thou art a holy being, found in the shape of a deer. Since Thou pleadest for this bad man, I shall give him the reward he coveted as he has made me acquainted with Thee. And Thou shalt have freedom to go anywhere Thou choosest and nobody shall hurt Thee." The Bodisāttva answered: "I accept this grant of freedom and I await the orders of the King."

The king but the Kuru-Deer on his royal chariot and, bowing down to him, conducted him in procession to his capital. Here he was placed on the royal throne, and before his queen and retinue the king asked the deer to preach the Law to them. Then the deer in a sweet voice preached to them about "Mercy to all creatures."

He said: "If men would consider the animals their younger brothers, then all wickedness would disappear in the world. The want of mercy is the cause of trouble. Mercy will bring rich fruits, as fruitful rain does to vegetation. Mercy destroys the desire for injuring any creature and is the seed of other virtues. A merciful person is loved and esteemed by everybody. His mind is so filled with merey that anger and passion cannot blaze in him. In mercy the whole Law of Righteousness is contained."

Thus the Bodhisattva taught the Law of Righteousness a long time ere he became the Buddha. And the king and his people took the words to their hearts and from that time the killing of animals and birds was forbidden.

VII.

THE STORY OF THE GREAT APE

It is said that once upon a time the Bodhisattva lived in the shape of a mighty ape. This ape lived on that part of the Himalayas, where magnificent forests with trees laden with fruit covered all the sides of the mountain. Here water-falls dashed down the precipices, and different coloured flowers, spreading their yellow, blue and lilac blossoms, scented the balmy air with fragrance

Here the Bodhisattva, quite content with the leaves and roots and fruits with which the beautiful forest furnished him, lived the life of an ascetic. Even though imprisoned in the body of a huge monkey, the Bodhisattva had not lost the consciousness of being righteous-

and compassionate, and, whenever he could help or teach any of the animals living in his neighbourhood, he did so. Men seldom came to these regions of solemn beauty and peace.

But one day a man was in search of one of his cows which had gone astray, and wandering in all directions in his vain search he lost his way altogether in this immense forest. Further and further he wandered, till at last he sank down under a tree exhausted by hunger, thirst, and grief for his lost cow, giving up hope for ever finding his way back to his village.

Looking around, he saw near him a number of ripe tinduka fruits lying among the grass and, being very hungry, he ate them. Then he wondered where the tree stood from which they had fallen, and he saw quite near him a tinduka-tree, which was growing near a precipice, down which there rushed a sparkling waterfall. He climbed up into the tree and saw one branch loaded with ripe fruit hanging just above the precipice. He climbed on to this branch and was eating the fruits quite contentedly, when the branch broke and he fell with it down the precipice.

He would certainly have been killed by the fall if the branch had not fallen into the water, and so, only drenched and frightened, he crawled out of the water and found himself at the bottom of a pit-like hole.

Steep rocks, like walls, made his ascent up the precipice impossible. He gave up hope of ever getting up and he saw death by starvation before him. He burst into tears of despair and lamented his sad fate: "Oh why did I fall into this dreadful hole?" he cried. "Nobody is with me, except swarms of mosquitos, feeding on my blood. Nobody can find me here but Death. Never shall I see again the beauty of the world above me."

For several days and nights the poor man remained in this pit. He ate the tinduka fruits which had fallen down with him and drank from the waterfall, but soon also the fruits were finished and starvation threatened him.

Just at this time, the Bodhisattva, in the shape of the Great Monkey, had come near the same tinduka tree from which the man had fallen down the precipice, and while he was plucking some fruit for his food, he heard a sound come out of the hole below him. Looking down he saw a miserable, emaciated, pale man lying down there. He stopped at once plucking the fruits and in a human voice said: "Who art thou, lying at the bottom of this chasm whence no man can return?"

When the man, looking up to the tree from which these words came, saw the big money, he bent his knees and, folding his hands in prayer, said with a trembling voice: "Great being there above me, I am a man and have fallen into this hole while eating the fruits on that very tree upon which thou sittest. I implore thee, protector of monkeys, be my protector also." The Bodhisattva, full of compassion, comforted the man and answered:

"Do not fear. That which your relatives would do if they were here, I will do: only have a little patience.

He threw down for the man some of the tindukas, so that he could stay his hunger and then the monkey jumped down the tree. He first searched for a place where he could get down the precipice, and then put a stone of a man's weight on his back, in order to try his strength and see whether he could carry the man on his back out of the pit. After trying his strength in this way, the monkey climbed down to the man and said kindly: "Climb on my back and hold tight to me, so that I may carry you out of this pit-hole by means of my body, which is ready to help you out of your trouble."

The man, bowing down to the Bodhisattva in gratitude, did what he was told, and the monkey, with great trouble and almost breaking down under the weight of the man on his back, succeeded in climbing to the top of the precipice, where he sank down almost completely exhausted on a broad slab of rock: "I must rest here and sleep, for my body is tired to death," he said to the rescued man. "Watch at my side, for many wild beasts are living around here which might attack me while I am asleep. Wake me if anything unusual happens."

The man assured him that he would guard his rescuer faithfully and the tired monkey fell fast asleep.

While the man was watching by the side of the monkey, he looked at his own emaciated body and wicked thoughts came into his mind; "There are only fruits and roots for me here;" he said to himself, "how can I gain strength and vigour on them and find my way home to my village? If I could kill this monkey, his flesh would give me more strength. It is true he has been good to me, but he is only a monkey and I am a man, and it is said that in time of distress one may feed on flesh."

And the man forgot gratitude and compassion in his greed and took a heavy stone and let it fall on the head of the sleeping monkey in order to kill him. But his trembling and weak hands could not deal the death-blow. The stone, instead of killing the monkey, awakened him after bruising his head on one side and then fell to the ground.

The monkey jumped up and looked round to find out who had injured him thus. He could not see anybody else but the man, whom he had saved and who stood before him with an ashy-pale face and down cast eyes, the beads of perspiration falling down from him. So it was he who had tried to kill his rescuer!

But this did not make the monkey angry; it did not make him revengeful, but full of compassion and with tears in his eyes the Bodhisattva said: "Friend, how has it been possible for thee, a man, to do this vile deed? Oughtest thou not to have defended me from any enemy who might try to injure me? I felt a little proud that I had done a thing which was difficult to do, but thou hast done something very much more difficult than I have done, and my pride is gone. After I brought thee out of one abyss, thou hast fallen into another. Shame upon thy ignorance, which has made thee so vile. Thou hast ruined thy good name, and virtue has flown from thee. Nobody can trust thee any more. It is not my wound that pains me, but my mind is full of pain, to think that I have produced these evil thoughts in thee. I cannot take away this sin from thee! Come with me now. I will conduct thee upon the right path, which will bring thee to thine own people. Thou mightest lose thy way and be killed by some beast, and so the labour I spent on thee would be lost. But remember to go on in front of me, for I cannot trust thee."

The Bodhisattva conducted the miserable man to the end of the forest and bid him good-bye and asked him not to do any more evil actions, for he said: "The consequences of evil actions are very painful."

Then the Bodhisattva went back to his residence in the forest and lived in peace.

But the miserable man, tormented by remorse, had no rest any more. He did not dare return to his home, for at once his body became covered with a kind of leprosy, making his skin change, and it became covered with spots. Wherever he went, he was driven away with clubs and evil words, as he was considered a demon by the frightened people. From that time he had to live in the forest.

Once a king saw him and asked him: "Are you a demon or a goblin?" * The man answered, "I am a man, although disfigured by the disease brought on myself as punishment for my evil deeds! It is the fruit of my ingratitude to the greatest friend I ever had, who rescued me from the jaws of Death and whom I betrayed. Take this dreadful condition in which your Majesty finds me as a warning and follow the Path of Righteousness and Compassion, and happiness will follow."

This story teaches that the Bodhisattva, in this shape of a monkey, still remembered the Law of Compassion through all his previous births and through all the long ages or yugas, † though earth and sea had often been destroyed.

It is said that the ungrateful man became later on, in the last earth life of the Buddha his cousin Devadatta, and then too he tried to kill Him, but again failed and died miserably. Yet even Devadatta, it is said, will one day be a Paccheka Buddha.

---

* Wood-devil. † Yuga—World-period.

VIII.

THE STORY OF THE GOLDEN SWANS.

Once, long long ago, it is said that the Bodhisattva was born as the king of the swans. He was at the head of a very large tribe and lived with his subjects on the wonderful lake Mânasa, which is supposed to exist on the Mountain Kailâsa in the Himâlayas.

The name of the Bodhisattva, when he was the king of the swans, was Dhritarâshtra and his Commander-in-Chief was called Summakha.*

The king and his friend were very much superior to the other swans and both used to teach the tribe, as a teacher and his best disciple teach the other pupils, or as a father and his eldest son teach the younger children. Thus carefully taught, the whole tribe of swans became famous through the whole land on account of their peaceful and just behaviour towards all other birds and animals.

The lake on which they dwelt was exceedingly beautiful. Flowering trees, which reflected their beauty in the clear waters of the lake, surrounded its border, and pink and blue lotuses peeped out of the water, resting on their green leaves like the sweet smiling face of a child on

---

* He is said to have been Ananda who was afterwards the favourite pupil of the Bodhisattva in his last incarnation on earth.

its cushion. Here oported the swans in groups or in a mass together, looking like snow-white clouds on the blue sky.

The two leaders of these swans looked so majestic, when they were at the head of their flock, or when they were teaching, that their fame spread everywhere and it was said that they surely had only the shape of swans, but must in reality be humau beings.

At this time there lived in Benares a king with the name of Brahmadatta. He had heard his people talk about the two wonderful swans, who lived with their tribe of swans on the magnificent lake of Mânasa. He became very curious to see these two birds and he asked his ministers to make a plan, so that he could see at least these two swans. The ministers answered the king that there was only one possibility of getting a sight of the swans and that was it the king would have a lake constructed, which would surpass in beauty even the lake Mânasa. Then, they thought, the swans might be induced to leave their present abode and come to live on the king's lake.

The king was pleased with this proposal and he at once ordered that in one of the forests, not too far from his capital, a magnificent lake should be made.

So a pond was widened and deepened, and waterlilies and lotuses began to bloom in the new lake, flowering bushes and trees smiled at their reflections in the clear water and strewed the pollen of their flowers like a carpet on its borders. Fishes sported in the water. Elephants, delighting in the clearness and freshness of the water, dipped their trunks into it and bathed their huge bodies, with cascades of spray which fell like silver pearls into the lake. In the nights the moon and the stars shone upon the clear lake and there was not its equal anywhere.

Every-day a tom-tom beater proclaimed that king Brahmadatta was pleased to give this lake, with all it contained and the land surrounding it, as a present to all birds, to whom he granted perfect safety.

So the birds came, cranes and flamingos and other—water birds, and the little singing-birds filled the branches of the trees, which stood on the shores of the lake. Bees hummed over the flowers, and peacocks spread their tails and danced in delight round the lake and pheasants peeped through the bushes and all was peace and happiness. No fowler or fisherman came near.

"But where are the wonderful swans, for whom I had this fair lake created?" said king Brahmadatta one day, when he looked at the lake and saw many birds, but not any swans. "They will come," answered the ministers, "a little later in the season, when they are accustomed to fly about."

So the king waited.

One day when the rain clouds had disappeared from the dark sky, and when the earth and the lake Mânasa smiled in beauty and radiance, some pairs of young swans from the tribe of the Bodhisattva lifted themselves on their wings for a long flight. They passed over towns and forests and there they saw in a beautiful valley, surrounded by lovely trees, a glittering sheet of water.

"Let us have a swim on that lake, which looks as lovely as our own home," said one of the swans, and all of them alighted.

To their surprise they found all kinds of water-birds on this lake, but no swans, and looking around they saw the *sal*, *kadamba*, the *arjiena* and *keteka* trees full of merry singing birds. They saw the peacocks and pheasants, and all were happy and content and no fear disturbed their innocent pleasures. They were so delighted with all they saw, that they wished that all their friends could enjoy the beautiful lake too.

They remained for some time there so that they might tell their friends all they saw and induce their king to come here with the whole flock. They themselves heard by the tom tom proclamation that there was safety for all birds on and round the lake and that made them happy.

The swans remained till the beginning of the rainy reason and when the sky for the first time filled with clouds, and the lightning began to flash, gilding the grey clouds with sudden beauty; when the thunder just rolled gently in the distance and the fresh winds began to blow, the swans flew back to their home and their own tribe.

They were full of news when they saw their companions, and they gave such a glorious description of the lake constructed by the king Brahmadatta, that their king Dhritarâshtra heard about it.

So they were called before him and after they had described the beauty of the lake they had dwelt on for a short time, and told how all birds had freedom there and were protected by the proclamation of king Brahmadatta, all the swans were anxious to go there after the rainy season should be over.

But the king turned to his wise counsellor Sumakha and asked for his advice in this affair. And Sumakha shook his head and said: "Your Majesty, I do not trust man, and I fear that the beauty of this place has been created as a trap for your Majesty. Birds and animals express their true feelings by their cries, but men are the only animals who disguise their feelings by saying something different from what they really mean. If the excursion to this new lake has to be made, then I would advise that we stay only for a short time and do not take up our residence there altogether."

The swans were not satisfied with these words and they requested their king again and again to take them to the beautiful lake near Benares and to remain there. At last the king of the swans consented to an excursion to the much talked of lake, and one full-moon night Dhritaräshtra and Sumakha, at the head of the flock of swans from the Manasa lake, began their flight towards Benares. Arrived at the lake all were delighted with it and in a short time most of the swans had almost forgotten their home and they were very happy and content on the new lake with its beautiful surroundings They had heard the proclamation of safety and they believed themselves in a haven of rest and security.

But the guardians of the lake reported to king Brahmadatta that a number of swans had arrived and that two of them shone out in beauty and size among them so they thought that these must be the very swans whom the king wanted to see.

When king Brahmadatta heard this he was very glad and he called the best of his fowlers and asked him to catch these two great swans. The fowler watched the two leaders of the swans, and in those places which they most frequented he set some strong snares, which were to catch their feet, when they were swimming about.

Not suspecting anything and trusting to the words of the king's proclamation the Bodhisattva and his friend were enjoying themselves among the lotuses of the lake, when the foot of Dhritarashtra got entangled in a snare. In order to warn the other

The fowler and the swans.

swans of danger, he announced by a certain cry that he had been caught and the swans with a cry of terror flew up into the air. Only Sumakha stayed at the side of his Master and would not move.

The Bodhisatta urged his friend to leave him as he could not help him, but Sumakha answered "Whatever thy fate is, my Master, that shall be mine also. I always attend on thee in thy prosperity and I will not leave thee in thy distress." The Bodhisattva answered: "My fate will be the kitchen, as is the fate of birds ensnared. Why should you follow me there? And what advantage will there be in the death of both of us?"

Sumakha answered: "The law of Righteousness teaches that one may not leave one's friend in distress, even for the sake of saving one's own life!" "That you have proved" answered the Bodhisatta, "and therefore, I give you leave now to fly away. Besides you must fill my place in my kingdom, as you are wise."

While they were thus talking with each other, the fowler came and, seeing that all the swans had flown away except two, he thought at once that they must have been caught, so he rushed on them like father Death himself.

When he found that only one was caught and the other stayed with him of his own free will, he was very much astonished and he said to Sumakha: "I wonder why this bird, which has his liberty does not use it and fly away?"

To the astonishment of the fowler the swan answered: "How is it that thou wonderest that I do not fly away at thy approach, although I am not snared like my companion who is in thy power? Dost thou not know that his virtues have bound my heart to him with stronger ties than thy snares have bound his foot?"

Full of admiration the fowler said: "What is this bird to thee? All the other swans have fled, but thou remainest?" Sumakha replied: "He is my king, my friend, whom I love more than my own life. How could I leave him, when he is in distress?"

The fowler was quite touched by the words he heard and he said: "I do not want both of you, so fly away and join your relations."

Sumakha answered: "If you want only one of us, take me. Our bodies are almost alike and our age is the same. Set my king free and take me instead of him and thus thou wilt not lose thy profit. Tie me ere thou loosest the king, if thou dost not trust me, and thus thou wilt be sure of me The gratitude of all the swans will be thine, if they see their beloved king come back to them."

The fowler, although accustomed to his cruel business, was so touched by the love manifested by the one bird for the other that, forgetting the order of the king to catch these swans, he said, lifting his hands in homage to the bird: "If such faithfulness were shown among men, it would be called a wonder. I must pay my reverence to thee, for how could I be cruel to the one for whom thou art willing to give thine own life? I will set thy Master free."

With these words, the fowler, asking the pardon of the Bodhisattva for ensnaring him, untied the snare."

With a grateful look at the man, Sumakha said: "Mayest thou, who hast gladdened my heart by the release of the king of the swans, be happy with thy relatives and friends for thousands of years to come. But in order not to be punished by the king, take both of us to him and show us to him, carrying us untied in two open baskets. The king surely will reward thee with a rich gift."

After some hesitation the fowler took the two famous swans to king Brahmadatta, who was delighted to see them and who was astonished at their beauty and wondered why they suffered themselves to be brought to him untied and unhurt. Then the fowler told the king the whole story, and how he was so overcome by the human words of the bird and by his willingness to sacrifice himself for his master that he set him free.

"Out of gratitude" continued the fowler, "the swan proposed that I should take him and his companion to you, so that I might get a reward for my trouble. Whoever they may be, under the shape of swans, they must be great human beings, that they can move me to such tenderness, cruel and coarse man that I am."

The king could hardly believe his ears, and with great joy he had a golden throne erected for the Bodhisattva and a bamboo seat for his minister. Then the Bodhisattva, with a voice as sweet as the evening breeze, said to the king : "Thy mind and body are healthy, king, are they not ? Thou art merciful and just, thou art prosperous, thou lovest thy religion and thy subjects, and thou art a hero of much courage. What is thy wish now ?"

The king answered : "My happiness, is now complete, as I have had the gladness of seeing your holy persons. But tell me, did the fowler hurt Thee by his snares ?"

The swan answered : "The fowler has not hurt me with his snare nor with his words. May our arrival bring him happiness, as it has brought happiness to Thee, O King !"

During the whole night the king of the Swans conversed with king Bramadatta and the wise swan Sumakha also had his say.

Delighted with all the advice he received, the king listened. And when at dawn the golden swan said that he must now return to his mourning subjects, king Brahmadatta, although filled with grief, allowed both of the fair creatures to depart.

The fowler, of course, became rich through the gifts of the king and he never again ensnared birds.

Once more the Bodhisattva returned to king Brahmadatta with his faithful friend Sumakha, bringing the whole company of swans with him, thus showing their gratitude to the king for releasing their Master. Then the golden swan taught the Law of Righteousness to king Brahmadatta, who honoured the Bodhisattva in return by bowing low and by following in the Path of Righteousness.

IX.

THE STORY OF THE CARABHA DEER

Once in the succession of lives through which the Bodhisattva had to pass on his way to Buddhahood, it is said that he was a Carabha Deer. He was not one of the kind of common deer, but stronger and statelier than all others and very much wiser. He lived in a forest far away from human habitations, and thick grass covered the edible roots and plants where no tracks of passing vehicles were to be found.

The Bodhisattva had not only a strong and healthy body, but he had also a shining skin, beautiful to look at. He lived like an ascetic on roots, leaves and water, and, having a heart full of compassion, he was kind to any animal that was in distress. Although he had the shape of an animal, he had the intellect of a man.

One day the king who was the ruler of this part of the country went out on a hunting expedition. Sitting on his swift horse he had his bow and arrow ready for shooting, when he saw the Bodhisattva in the shape of the beautiful Carabha deer. The Bodhisattva could have withstood the king, but as he had given up all acts of violence he took to flight and, being very swift, the king's horse had to run very fast in pursuit.

The king, bent on shooting the beautiful animal, did not pay any attention to the surrounding forest, and he did not see a great chasm over which the deer jumped as easily, as if it were a small brook. The horse, seeing the chasm before him, came to such a sudden stand-still, while getting ready for the leap, that the king was thrown head over heels into the hole.

When the Carabha Deer, running away, did not hear the trampling of the horse's hoofs behind him any more, he looked round and saw the riderless horse standing on the opposite side of the big hole and looking down into its depths.

The Bodhisattva at once thought that the king must have fallen into the hole, as there was no probability that he would have dismounted in the depth of the forest in order to hunt on foot: "If the king has not killed himself, falling down that pit," thought the deer, "he will need some help to get out of it and I must help him." And moved by compassion

Scenes from the story of the Carabha Deer.

he turned back and looked down into the hole and saw the king struggling there, endeavouring to climb up, in which effort he evidently was not succeeding as the sides of the hole were steep and slippery.

The Bodhisattva entirely forgot that the king was his enemy, who had tried just a little while ago to kill him, and bending down over the precipice he said with a human voice: "I hope Your Majesty has not got hurt? I hope no bones are broken? I am no goblin, but only a forest animal, living on your grass and leaves and water. You are in your own realm. Do not fear, I have the strength to help you out of your distress. Trust me and give me your orders."

The king was very much astonished and ashamed, when he heard these kind words from the deer, whom he had pursued just a little while ago, and he answered very kindly: "My body has not been injured very severely by the fall into this wretched hole, being protected by my armour. The pain I have does not hurt me as much as the pain I feel in mistaking you for an ordinary animal, misguided by your appearance. Pray pardon me."

The deer being satisfied that the king accepted his offered help, began to try whether he could carry a man's weight by putting a heavy stone on his back and climbing with it. When he found that he was strong enough, he went down into the hole and said to the king: "May Your Majesty deign to use me as your horse for a while. I am strong enough and willing to carry you out of this pit." The king mounted the deer's back and with wonderful strength and skilfulness he carried him up.

The deer now wanted to retire to the forest again, but the king embracing him said : " My life, which has been saved through you, is at your disposal. Come with me to my capital and reside there if you like. Here in the forest you may be chased by hunters or molested by beasts."

The Bodhisattva was very much pleased at the words of the king and he said : " I see you are a lover of virtue and justice. I thank you for your offer ; but the habits of forest animals are different from those of men, and I prefer to stay in the forest. But if your Majesty would like to do something pleasant to me, then promise me never to hunt any more in all your life. Animals have fear and horror (like human beings) of being hunted. So do you have pity on them. Think that animals, just as men, like happiness and quiet, and therefore do not do to them what would be disagreeable to yourself.

" Destroy the evil which yet remains in you. Your meritorious actions have gained you the high office of king. Add more meritorious actions, which are the means of obtaining glory and happiness. Your righteousness will increase the happiness of your subjects and they will become more virtuous also."

The king accepted the teachings of the

Bodhisattva and from this time no more hunting was done in his realm.

The Carabha deer retired again into the forest where no hunter disturbed his peace.

This story teaches compassion towards animals and shows that, when in distress, even a former enemy should be helped out of compassion by the very one who has been injured by him.

X.

THE STORY OF THE GREAT MONKEY

Somewhere in the Himalayas there was a forest which was wonderfully fertile. Hundreds of trees, all of different kinds, were found there, and health-giving herbs grew in abundance. Mountain streams were sparkling in crystal purity, joining with their laughing murmur the various songs of the birds, which lived happily in the branches of the trees.

Here in the middle of the forest, somewhat away from other trees, stood a magnificent peepul-tree. It was much taller than the other forest trees and its branches reached far out. When it was covered with its white blossoms, it looked like a mass of white clouds, overtowering all other trees.

In this grand tree there lived at that time the Bodhisattva in the shape of an immense monkey. By his wisdom he had become the leader of a whole tribe of monkeys, who considered him their king. He was larger than any of the other monkeys, and, although in the shape of an animal, he possessed human wisdom, and his charity and compassion were well-known among the animals.

His tribe lived with him in this magnificent peepul-tree, and their principal food consisted of the delicious fruits, which grew abundantly on this king of trees. One of the branches of this tree was hanging over the river Ganges, which flowed near this forest, and the monkey-king knowing that trouble would come to the monkey-tribe if one of the fruits should fall into the river and be carried away towards the habitations of people, ordered his monkeys to be very careful to destroy the buds of all the fruits, which were growing on this overhanging branch.

His orders were always faithfully carried out. But one year, when the monkeys cleared away the fruit-buds they overlooked one and it grew into a lovely fruit, which ripened unobserved by them.

When it was quite ripe and soft, the stalk loosened and it fell into the river. It was carried down till it came near Benares, and got entangled in the corner of a fence which had been erected in the river to divide off a bathing place for the king and his wives.

The King hears about the fruit.

The fruit is brought to the King.

Here it remained stuck and it had such a strong and delicious smell, that the ladies who were bathing wondered where the sweet scent came from, which was much stronger than all their ointments and the garlands of sweet smelling flowers which they wore. At last one of them discovered the ripe peepul-fruit and brought it to the king. The king had it examined by his physician, who declared that the taste of it was just as delicious as the smell.

The king himself became as curious as his wives about this fruit as he had never seen it before and when they tasted it, they all declared that they had never eaten anything so delicious. The king said : "I am a king and this is just the right food for kings and I must find out where this fruit comes from. It cannot have come from very far, for it is perfectly fresh and not injured or rotten. The tree must stand near the river too, otherwise it would have been hurt by the fall, I shall find out where it grows"

So he called together his army and he searched the forest near Benares. He had to make his way through the jungle and at last they saw before them an immense peepul-tree upon which a host of monkeys were sitting eating fruits. When they came nearer, the whole atmosphere was filled with fragrance, and the king recognised the same scent which had delighted him and his wives, from the fruit which had been carried down the Ganges to his bathing-place.

The king was quite sure that this was the tree he was searching for, and when he saw that many hundreds of monkeys were eating the fruits which he wanted to have, he ordered his soldiers to destroy them.

The poor monkeys were frightened to death, when they saw the soldiers shooting arrows and throwing clubs and stones at them. They looked helplessly and pleadingly at their king, who was contemplating what he could do to save his poor subjects. He had seen the approach of the army and he was filled with compassion and he told them to be comforted for he would save them. Then he sprang up to the top of the tree and made a mighty leap, which landed him on a mountain peak too far away for the ordinary monkeys to reach, but which he, with his extraordinary strength and size could just gain. Now the Bodhisattva searched for a tall bamboo, long enough to reach across the space between the mountain and his tree.

He found one deep-rooted, strong and tall, and fastening the top of it to his feet he dared the leap again to his tree. But this time it was much more difficult to jump, as he was hindered by the bamboo, the end of which was fastened on his feet. But the Bodhisattva did not hesitate, for it meant life or death for his tribe. He jumped and he could just catch hold of the nearest overhanging branch of the big peepul-tree. But he clutched the branch tightly and, as the bamboo was fastened strongly on to his feet, he had thus made a

The Monkey-King called out to the monkeys to use the bridge.

bridge for his monkeys to the mountain side.

He called out to them to use this bridge for their escape, and the frightened animals, forgetting that part of this bridge was formed of the body of their king, wildly rushed over his body to the peak and trampled on the body of the Bodhisattva in such a way that he was fatally injured.

He did not mind the pains he suffered; but, when all the monkeys had escaped, he fainted.

In the meanwhile the king and his army had watched this wonderful performance, and the king would not allow his soldiers to shoot at the valiant monkey-king, who was sacrificing himself for his tribe.

When the monkeys had all escaped he ordered a canopy to be made with four sticks which were planted in the ground, just under the branch on which the monkey-king hung and two of his best archers had to sever the branch and the tied bamboo at the same time, so that the monkey-king should fall down into the cloth of the canopy without being injured. He had lost consciousness altogether and did not know what happened.

The king had the monkey's wounds attended to carefully and when the Bodhisattva opened his eyes he found himself on a soft couch and the king bending over him. With admiration in his eyes the king asked the Bodhisattva gently : "How is it that thou hast sacrificed thy body for the welfare of the monkeys?

What art thou to them? There must be a very strong tie of friendship between thee and them for thee to do such a thing."

The Bodhisattva in a feeble voice answered: "I was their ruler, and their father, and therefore I had to help them in their trouble."

"But the ministers and attendants have to serve and help the king, not the king serve them", said the king. "Well, that is political wisdom, oh King," answered the Bodhisattva, "but in this case they all looked up to me for help, for I was the only one who could help them and my heart, full of compassion, prompted me to make those two leaps which saved them all. If I had thought of myself and not of them, they would have been lost."

The king admired the great compassion of the king of the monkeys and he asked: "But what benefit hast thou got by despising thy own welfare?" "The Bodhisattva answered: "I know my body is broken and my strength is gone, but my mind has gained clearness since I have helped those who were in distress. I bear the pains I suffer as a hero in war the laurels he gains, and my approaching death is to me like going to a great festival. I have not only gained the regard of my tribe, but a great king is honouring me and my fame will live after me. The mercy I have showed for my subjects will be a lesson also to thee. And great king "thou wilt rule in righteousness over thy people and gain merit, wealth, and glory. Then thou wilt be like the holy king of old who only ruled with love and compassion over his people."

The king had listened with the humility of a pupil to the dying monkey-king, who overcome by the pains of his sacrifice for his tribe, left his earthly body *and mounted to heaven!*

Such was the glorious death of the Bodhisattva in the shape of a monkey, who taught that, by sacrificing his body for the salvation of his subjects, a ruler must think of their needs when they are in misery, and not of his own body.

XI.

THE STORY OF THE WHITE ELEPHANT.

Once the Bodhisattva lived as a huge white elephant in a large forest, which was surrounded on three sides by a desert. Mountain ridges bordered the one side of this enormous forest and a large lake, covered with lotuses of every kind, made it an agreeable and desirable abode. This forest was little known by people and human voice was hardly ever heard under the shade of the ancient trees, which united their high branches as in an embrace and this formed an immense green hall. Here the king of the elephants lived in solitary grandeur. The leaves and branches of the trees were his food and the water of the lotus-lake his drink.

One day the white elephant was wandering about near the border of the forest towards the wilderness, when he heard in the distance the voices of many people, who seemed to be in great trouble. He listened intently and it seemed to him as if this crowd of people must have got lost in the desert, as the noise he heard seemed to be cries of distress.

"May be these people are lost in the desert, or perhaps banished by the command of a king and they are perishing of hunger and thirst, I must run to them and see what I can do for them," thought the compassionate elephant. And quickly he ran in the direction whence came the distressing noise.

As the desert was bare of trees, he could see very far and he discovered in the distance a number of people, who were crying and groaning, evidently overcome by hunger, thirst and fatigue.

These people, about seven-hundred in all, at first became frightened when they saw a big white elephant running towards them. But as they were too weak to run away they gave up hope of life all thinking that this huge king of the forest could very easily trample them to death.

When the Bodhisattva, in the shape of the elephant, saw their terror, he called out in a gentle human voice : "Fear not! Do not be afraid, no harm will come to you from me."

The unhappy people looked upon the huge white elephant in awe and fear, but they saw his kind eyes and heard his gentle voice and became less afraid.

Lifting up, his trunk as if in greeting, the elephant said to them "How did you come to this desolate place? What brought you here, so far away from human society?" "Alas," said one of the unfortunate people, "we have been driven away from our country by our angry king, one thousand souls banished into the desert to die Three hundred of us have already perished and we remaining seven hundred await death here, as we are too exhausted to go much further, and we are famished through want of drink and food. Can you help us? Can you show us the way to some shelter and food?"

The elephant answered: "My heart feels sad for you. Your king cannot have been taught the miseries of starvation and death, otherwise he could not have sent you out thus into the desert. Oh! the misery of ignorance!" Saying these words the compassionate elephant thought: "How can I help these poor miserable, starving people who look up to me for assistance. Even if they should reach my forest, how could they find enough food there? If I gave up my body to them they might be sustained by my flesh, till they could reach the mountains, settle down and begin a new life. I will help them by giving them my body, which will be like a raft in the sea of their misery!"

While the elephant was thus thinking how he could help this unhappy crowd of starving people, they begged him with uplifted hands to show them a place where they could find shelter, drink and food.

The elephant looked at them with tears of compassion in his eyes, lifted up his trunk and pointing towards the direction of the mountain ridge he said: "Follow the direction which I point out to you. You will find a forest and a large lake covered with lotuses. Quench your thirst and rest and when you are able to go on, you will find near the lake at the foot of the mountain, the corpse of an elephant, just perished by falling from the mountain ridge. Take his flesh and satisfy your hunger, take the remainder as provisions on your road and fill the entrails of his body with water, using them for water-bags. Thus provisioned you will easily be able to reach the valley behind the mountain, where you can settle down and live contentedly, as it has plenty of food and drink. Follow my advice and begin your search for your safety at once."

With these comforting words the white elephant ran off to reach the mountain-ridge from another side. He had resolved that his favourite lotus-lake should furnish drink for the exhausted, and that his body should be used as food for the starving.

Arrived on the top of the mountain with a precipice before him, the white elephant halted for a moment and thought: "Even though I do not reach Nirvana now by sacrificing myself for this starving people, if I can help them now by feeding their bodies, I may deliver them in future times out of the wilderness of Samsara.*"

With a glad heart the elephant threw himself down the precipice, and it is said that while falling, his body shone like an autumn cloud or like the moon sinking with its disc turned upside down behind the mountain.

The mountain trembled and the earth shook. Mara the tempter was troubled and the Devas of the forest waved their slender green arms in astonishment, pointing upwards and showering flowers down on the crushed body of the king of animals.

Hymns of praise and adoration filled the air, while the forest-devas surrounded the fallen body, bowing their heads devotedly before the one who had sacrificed himself thus willingly.

Meanwhile the seven hundred starving people had followed the directions given them by the white elephant and they found the lotus-lake easily. Then they quenched their thirst and refreshed their famished bodies with the cool water and ate greedily the roots of the lotuses.

After resting a while they went in search of the corpse of an elephant, as they had been

---

* Samsara is, according to Buddhist teachings, the whirl pool of life and being born again and again.

told and they saw not far from the lake the body of an elephant, evidently dead just a short time ago. The body looked just like a mountain covered with flowers and they stood back in awe and some exclaimed: "Does not this look like the king of the elephants who came to us and advised us how to get out of our trouble?" Others cried: "Oh, surely we cannot use as food the body of him who has delivered us out of our misery?" "Yes, yes, he is the same," said some others, "just look at the two magnificent tusks, white as snow, but now covered with the dust of the mountain and look at the fingerlike tip of the large trunk, with which he showed us the right way. So he has sacrificed his body for us, what friendship! what surpassing compassion!" cried out a few. "He surely is on the way to the perfecting of self! Who could have been his teacher in this forest? We cannot feed on the body of one who has sacrificed himself. We must cremate him with the honours due to a king!"

"But, said some, whose minds were stronger, he has directed us and told us to feed on his body in order to save ourselves from starvation: let us follow his directions in every thing, for otherwise the sacrifice of his body for us would be in vain. He has sacrified all he had for the feeding of his guests, and if we do not accept his gift, he will have made that sacrifice in vain."

" Let us do his bidding and then burn the remains as if they were those of our relatives

Reverence paid to the statue of the White Elephant.

and worship him, according to our own ideas."

So they accepted the gift and taking their food from his body, using his entrails as water-bags, they went on their way, after burning the remains of the elephant with all funeral rites due to a king.

They reached the fruitful valley behind the mountain ridge safely, and from that time they worshipped the statue of a white elephant, as their guide and protector.

The story of their rescue out of the desert was handed down from father to son, in the valley of the White-Elephant.

XII.

THE STORY OF THE HEAD OF A GUILD

In one of his births, the Bodhisattva was a merchant, who on account of his good Karma and great activity, had acquired a large fortune and became the Head of the Merchants' Guild* He was esteemed by everybody for his fairness in business and because of his great learning; he was consulted by the wise of his country, and even the king of the land in which the Bodhisattva lived knew of him and called him his friend.

---

* Guild is an association of Merchants or Tradesmen, united for the protection of their class and trade.

The heart of the rich merchant was full of love and charity for the poor, and no person in need ever left his house without receiving a gift.

One day, about meal time, when the Bodhisattva had just bathed and anointed his body, ready to partake of the food prepared for him by his wife and excellent cooks, a mendicant drew near the gate of the house, who, by his piety and learning had overcome all evil in himself. He now came to the wealthy merchant, begging for food, for he desired to increase the merchant's merit by so doing. The mendicant stood at the gateway quite silently, grasping his alms-bowl in his hands and gazing only a short distance in front of him, as monks must do, when they beg for their food.

But Mara,* the Evil One, could not bear to see the Bodhisattva enjoy the happiness of almsgiving, and, in order to prevent his doing so, he created, by his magical powers, the illusion of a deep chasm between the monk at the gate and the door of the Bodhisattva's house.

In this chasm he wished to imitate a hell, with dreadful sounds issuing therefrom, and flames shooting upwards, which were devouring hundreds of groaning people therein.

The Bodhisattva, not seeing this seeming hell, but only the holy monk standing at his

---

* Mara, The Tempter is in the East what the Devil is in the West.

The charitable merchant at his meal

The hell created by Mara.

gate, said to his wife, " My dear, go and bring to the mendicant at our gate a good portion of our food, so that he may bless us."

The wife at once collected the best portions of the food, and carried it out to the monk, but when she came to the chasm created by the Evil One, she shrank back in horror, and returned to her house in such a state of terror, that she could not even explain to her husband why she was unable to take the food to the patient mendicant.

The Bodhisattva, not wishing that the holy man should go from his gate without receiving refreshment, himself took the food to fill the begging bowl.

When the Bodhisattva drew near to the gate, he saw the awful chasm before him, and just as he was considering what he could do, Mara—the Tempter himself stood before him in a marvellous and divine form. He stood there supporting himself in the air, and addressed the rich merchant (the Bodhisattva) in a kind manner saying: "Householder, before you is Maha-roruvo, the great hell. This is the place reserved for those who, flattered by the praising voices of the beggars, are eager to give, because they have a vicious passion for charity. You injure your material property by giving it away, also you injure righteousness (dharma), because, in giving your wealth to the poor, you cannot give to the Gods. Therefore refrain from giving, so that you may not be swallowed up by the flame-tongued hell before you. Those who have ceased from the bad custom of giving obtain the rank of Devas. Therefore, use restraint and renounce charity which produces praise and flattery from those who habe received."

The Bodhisattva, however, recognised the Evil-One, and answered kindly but firmly: "This wish of mine to be charitable is an illness which has passed beyond the cure of medical art, and so, although you have spoken to me as a physician, advising the right cure for my illness, your advice comes too late. As to your teaching that wealth without charity can be called the path of virtue my weak human understanding cannot follow If, according to your teaching the *giver* goes to hell and the *receiver* to celestial abodes, then I will yet give more and thus help those who receive from me to go to Heaven. Not for my own happiness do I give in charity, but with the intention of helping the world."

Then Mara, the Tempter, spoke once more as if in earnestness aud said: "Decide for yourself. Either be happy and respected, or repent." The Bodhisattva said; "I would rather plunge into hell and be devoured by the flames, than neglect the beggaas who honour me in asking me for food."

After saying this the Bodhisattva, in spite of the terror of his family, stepped into the chasm before him. He knew that charity could not create evil; and lo! a white lotus sprang up under his feet, and lifted him up out of the surrounding hell. Then he filled the alms-bowl of the mendicant, with a heart full of joy and gladness.

The monk, in order to show his gratitude and power, raised himself into the air, where he shone with majesty, as shines the sun from behind a cloud. Thus he manifested the powers of the iddhis* he possessed.

When Mara, the Evil One, saw the holiness of the monk and felt his own power unable to deceive the merchant, he disappeared together with his hell, which he had created in hope of overcoming the virtues of the Bodhisattva.

This story teaches that the virtuous man should not be induced, even by threats, to desert the Path of Righteousness, and tread the way of evil.

XIII.

THE STORY OF THE HUNGRY TIGRESS.

Once upon a time, long ago, the Bodhisattva was born as a mighty and rich Brahman, who had gained a great reputation as a pure-minded and religious man.

* Iddhis—supernormal powers.

The Bodhisattva as a boy was very pious, and, as he was very quick in learning, he attained mastery of the eighteen branches of science, and all the arts which his Brahman teacher could teach him. Soon he knew more than his teachers, and was looked upon as almost a God of wisdom. He was very wealthy too, and fame and distinction became his.

But the Bodhisattva did not care for all these worldly things. His only delight was in the study of the Scriptures, and the wish grew greater and greater in him to renounce the world altogether.

In India, as you know perhaps, every Brahman passes through four stages in life – namely —childhood, youth (the stage of studentship) manhood, (when he becomes a householder,) and old age, which allows of retirement into the jungle.

When the Bodhisattva reached the stage when he ought to have become a householder, he refused to marry and live the life of attachment, but he retired instead into the jungle.

In the jungle, he lived a life of such purity, self control and calmness, that even the wild animals followed his example, and ceased injuring one another, and lived in friendship. All was peace and love around him.

His former companions and their friends wondered at the holiness of the young Brahman, and some of them left their homes, came to him and asked him to accept them as his pupils, which he did.

He then proceeded to teach them good conduct and purity of life. He also showed his pupils that much unhappiness comes to men, because they do not control their thoughts, but let them wander continually from one thing to another. The result of this is that their minds are full of the pleasures and anxieties of life which bind them down to this world. He therefore taught them to fix or concentrate their minds on holy things and so to keep themselves free from the world's temptations.

Thus in his disciples the Bodhisattva shut the doors of evil, and opened the road to happiness and salvation. Most of his pupils attained a high state of perfection through his teachings.

One day, the Bodhisattva was rambling with one of his disciples among the caves and shrubs of the mountain on which he dwelt. He was talking to him of the practice of yoga * or meditation, and of the happiness of renunciation, when he saw at the bottom of a precipice a young tigress, which was so weak from hunger that she could hardly walk. Her eyes were sunken and her body was as thin as a skeleton. Her young ones were close by, but she was so hungry, that she was ready to devour them, as she could not find anything to eat. She was snarling at them hoarsely.

Seeing all this suffering, the Bodhisattva was moved by compassion as a mountain is

* Yoga really means union with The One.

shaken by an earthquake, and he cried out to his companion Agita: "My son, behold the worthlessness of the Samsara! This animal contemplates feeding upon her own young ones; hunger is causing her to transgress love's law. Alas! the ferocity of self-love, which can cause a mother to wish to take her meal off the bodies of her own offspring! Go quickly, my son, in search of food to appease the hunger of this tigress, so that she may not injure her young ones. I also will try to stop her from doing this rash deed."

The disciple went away quickly to search for food for the tigress, but the Bodhisattva left alone thought: "Why should I search for flesh from the body of another, when I have my own body to offer? I cannot be happy whilst that tigress grieves, and I have the power to help her. If I remained indifferent to the grief of this harmful being, I should do evil, and my conscience would burn within me, as does a shrub which has caught fire. But if I throw myself down the precipice and kill my miserable body thus, the tigress will eat my body and her young ones will be saved. Thus I shall teach compassion to the world, and my wish to do good to another by the offering of my own body will be fulfilled, and I shall acquire great merit. This deed of mine is not prompted by ambitious motives, nor by the desire for glory, but only to secure the benefit for another. I take away the darkness of hunger from the tigress, even as the sun takes away the darkness of the earth by his light. The world will be taught compassion by my example."

Strengthened by these reflections, the Bodhi sattva, threw his body down the precipice before the tigress, who was just on the point of devouring her young ones The tigress heard the sound of the falling body, and, leaving her young ones, she crept to the spot where thr lifeless body of the Bodhisattva lay. With hungry eyes she looked at it, and at once began to devour it.

When Agita returned to the spot where he had left the Bodhisattva, he looked around in vain for him. At first he thought that the Bodhisattva had also gone in search of food for the tigress. He himself had found nothing that would satisfy the animal, and was at a loss what to do.

Presently he heard below him, the satisfied purr of the tigress, and looking down to find out what food the animal had found which was causing her to express her satisfaction in a purr-like growl, instead of the hungry snarl of some time ago he saw, to his great horror, the half-devoured body of his beloved teacher, and the tigress licking her paws in cantentment after her meal. Her young ones had again drawn near her and the tigress was looking fondly at them like a mother, instead of glaring like a ravenous beast ready to devour them. This sight, whic greeted Agita, was really an awful one.

At first he was almost overcome by grief at the loss of his dearly beloved teacher, but with his mind's eye he could see why the Bodhisattva had sacrificed his body. Throwing himself down in reverence, he exclaimed: "O how merciful was the Great-minded One to those in distress! How indifferent to His own welfare! How He has proved his immense love. Verily the creatures are no longer to be pitied, having gained Him as a protector. Mara surely, is now sighing in distress, being disturbed and in dread of defeat. All hail to that illustrious Great Being of boundless goodness—the refuge of all creatures!"

Agita returned to his fellow disciples and told them what had occurred. They all understood the great sacrifice the Bodhisattva had made of his body, and it is said that in admiration and veneration for his sacrifice the disciples, the Gandharvas,* the Yakshas,* the chiefs of the the Devas, even the snakes, covered the ground, where the bones of the precious body of the Bodhisattva were lying, with a profusion of flowers and sandal wood powder and worshipped them.

Thus did the Bodhisattva, who was to be the Buddha long ages afterward, show in this birth, his compassion for all creatures, by sacrificing his body to the wants of a hungry tigress.

---

* Gandharvas, Yakshas or Rakshasas, were Demons who could take any shape they wished and who were generally doing evil to human beings.

The King and the Queen.

XIV.

THE STORY OF THE SMALL PORTION OF GRUEL.

The following story of one of the lives of the Bodhisattva shows us that any gift, either great or small, given in faith to a worthy person, will produce a great result.

Once the Bodhisattwa was born as the king of Koshala, in India, having all the Virtues which a king ought to have, if he is to be the real father of his subjects.

He was just, energetic and learned; but one virtue shone forth, as a ray shines forth from its centre, the sun, and that was *great cheerfulness.*

This great cheerfulness had such a wonderful effect on his whole country, that everyone in it seemed happy and contented.

One day, when the king was attending to his religious duties, the recollection of one of his former incarnations came to his mind, and, moved greatly by what it revealed to him, he became more charitable than ever, Shramanas and Brahmans, beggars and old people, received gifts and also instruction from him.

Since the time when he had first looked back to his former lives the king had become more thoughtful than ever. In palace and in audience hall he was heard reciting verses which greatly aroused the curiosity of his people. The meaning of the verses was:—

"If anybody supplies the wants of the Holy Ones, even in a small way, the fruit of this action can never be small. I have heard this *said* before, now I *know* it to be true; I have seen what rich fruit has been produced by *a small portion of saltless coarse, brown gruel.*"

Now, all the Brahmans and attendants of the king became very curious as to the meaning of this peculiar utterance, and even the queen was anxious to understand it. So one day, in the audience hall before all the people, she asked the king to tell her what he meant by saying so often, "Such a rich fruit has been produced by a small portion of gruel."

The king, with a very kind look at his queen, answered her, "No wonder, my queen, that you are anxious to understand this strange saying. I will gladly explain it to you."

"Hearkea to my words, my beloved, and all my subjects present. One day, whilst engaged in deep meditation, I seemed to awake as from a sleep, and I saw that in my former existence on earth I had been a servant in this same town. I was then very poor, and had to earn my livelihood as a hired labourer.

"One day, as I was about to go out to look for work, in order to earn food for my family, I saw four Shramanas* going from house to house begging alms. They were holy men, and

* Young Monks, who have not been fully ordained.

The King tells the story of his former Incarnation.

thinking them poorer than myself, I took them to my house, and offered them the only food I had, and that was *a small dish of gruel.*

"Lo! my Queen and my people, out of that small beginning has grown all my present wealth. When I think of this, I recite these two stanzas, and rejoice that now I am able to welcome many holy people to my palace, and can perform many charitable deeds."

When the Queen heard this, her face shone with gladness, and she said, looking up to the King in admiration. "Mayest thou live long to be a father to thy people, thou who hast earned thy royal position by the former meditorious deed." The king answered. "I will endeavour, by doing good to my people, to walk on the path of happiness, and then my subjects also will love alms-giving, having heard the story of my former deed, which brought so much good to me. But, my Queen, thy face is aglow with a glory almost divine. Thou art shining like the sun amongst the stars, perchance thou too rememberest a happy deed done by thee in a former life?"

Looking up with wide-open eyes, as though she were looking into the far distance, the Queen replied:

"The remembrance of a former birth has come to me; I was a slave girl, and poor. A monk came to beg, and I gave him, with devotion in my heart, all that I had left of my meal. After that it seemed to me as if I were falling asleep, and as if I awoke as your Queen! You are most surely right in saying that "the reward of giving to a holy person is not small," for those were the words of the Muni* to whom I gave my meal when I was a slave girl in a former birth."

The people who were present, hearing the two stories told by the King and the Queen, were filled with admiration, amazement and piety, upon seeing what good Karma had resulted from the former good deeds of their king and queen, and a high esteem for meritorious actions was aroused in them.

The King, seeing this, urged on them the practice of charity and good conduct, which must always have the best results.

He also told them that almsgiving is a great virtue, which should always be cultivated. It cannot be taken away by thieves, nor can either fire or water destroy it. Almsgiving cleanses the heart from the sin of selfishness, and it is a means of relieving the fatigue of travel through Samsara.

All who heard the king, mediated on his words, altered their ways, and thereafter practised charity in the land of Koshala.

---

*Muni—a holy person, a teacher, a far-advanced monk.

The Queen as Slave-girl and the four Shramanas.

XV.

THE STORY OF AJASTYA

The following incarnation of the Bodhisattva shows how, as an ascetic, he practised constant liberality and charity, even to the point of starving himself, and that, even in this half-starved condition, he proved an inexhaustible mine of wise teachings.

The Bodhisattva was born this time in the family of an illustrious Brahman who was celebrated for his great purity and piety. His birth was considered a great boon to the family, and he was brought up as a strict Brahman, performing all prescribed sacraments and rites and learning the sacred texts of the Vedas with Angas, such as astronomy, mantrams, grammar, explanation of words, metrical science, etc. He rose quickly to fame and by rich gifts of his admirers he grew very wealthy. Now he distinguished himself not only by his learning, but also by his wealth, which he distributed freely to poor relations, friends and disciples.

When he reached the state of the householder, he did not feel quite content, for he saw that now he was expected to gather wealth and to accomplish numberless tasks, which hindered him in his strict religious duties.

His inner eye was opened and he saw that the renunciation of the world would bring him freedom from evil and would allow him to perform his religious duties in a perfect way, thus preparing the way to salvation.

So he retired from the household life and lived as an ascetic, throwing away his wealth freely, as if it were water.

But his admirers and those who wanted his teachings, still visited him, and, as he was wishing to detach himself entirely from the world, he retired to the Island of Kara, which was situated in the Southern Ocean. There was a beautiful lake in this Island, with fruit and flowering trees on its banks, and edible roots and health-giving herbs grew in abundance. Here the Bodhisattva built his hermitage and lived happy and contented as a strict ascetic, eating just enough to sustain life in his body.

When any guest arrived at his Hermitage of Penance, he always honoured him with the roots or fruits he had just gatherod for his own food, and with the clear water from the lake. And kind words of welcome and blessings always accompanied the simple food.

Thus the Bodhisattva lived a life of penanco and asceticism and even the animals in the forest honoured him as a Muni, lying at his feet, in reverence and obedience when they met him.

Now the fame and glory of the Bodhisattva's ascetic life came to the ears of the Deva-King Sakra, and he wanted to try the constancy of the Great-One, so he made all the fruits and roots which grew near the Hermitage of

Ajastya visited in his solitude.

Penance disappear. But the Bodhisattva, whose mind was fixed more on meditation than on thought of nourishment for his body, was content to boil leaves with the water of the lake, and he took this simple meal in contentment.

Then Sakra stripped all the trees and shrubs and grasses of their leaves, as the wind does in autumn, and the Bodhisattva was content to pick some of the yet fresh leaves and boil them for his food.

Sakra was more astonished than ever and almost angry that he could not make the Bodhisattva lose his contenment, and so he appeared before him as a Brahman, just at his meal-time.

The Bodhisattva met him kindly and invited him as a guest to enter his hermitage. Then with a glad face and kind words he presented him with the whole of the boiled leaves, which he had such trouble to find.

The Brahman finished the meal with satisfaction, and Agastya, the ascetic, had nothing but the joy of seeing his guest refreshed and pleased. It did not disturb his meditation at all; and all day and night he was filled with happiness.

On the second, third, fourth and fifth day Sakra appeared as a Brahman guest to the Bodhisattva, and every time he was greeted with the same kindness and joy, and every time he partook of the ascetic's food without leaving anything for him.

Sakra was amazed and became full of fear, that the Bodhisattva might, through his excessive penance and his extraordinary charitableness, enter the realm of the Devas and become their King, as he was greater even than tho Deva-King himself. So Sakra took on his beautiful celestial form and spoke to the ascetic : "Pray tell me why you have left your relatives, your family and friends, who loved you, and have come to this forest to live a life of penance without comfort?"

The Bodhisattva answered : "The coming back to earth brings sorrow; old age and disease brings sorrow and the neeessity of dying is a trouble to the mind. I am trying to solve the mystery of how to save all creatures from these evils. That is the reason. why I have left the world and live a life of meditation."

Sakra was very much pleased with this answer, for now he knew that the Bodhisattva did not aim at celestial glory and he said: "For the wisdom of this answer I give you a boon : choose anything you wish."

But the Bodhisattva had no desire for worldly things, as he had arrived at the state of contentment, and so he said: "May that fire of longing after a wife, children, and riches, which are desired by men, even after it has been gratified, never enter into my heart. That is the boon I ask."

This answer pleased Sakra more than ever, for he saw that Ajastya was entirely satisfied with his life of penance, and he said: "For this splendid utterance I give you gladly another boon. Speak, what shall it be?"

The Bodhisattva answered: "May the fire of hatred, through which a person loses wealth, caste and reputation, never enter into my heart."

Again Sakra applauded and said: "Rightly said! Fame comes to the one who has renounced the world, like a living woman, who attends to the wants of her husband, Accept another boon for these well spoken words."

Then Ajastya replied: "May I be spared the sight of a fool and the annoyance of living with him. This is the boon I ask."

"But why do you abhor the sight of a fool? Is it because foolishness is the root of evil?" asked Sakra. "A fool needs treatment, and you, a person full of compassion, should help him."

Ajastya answered: "If a fool were curable by any kind of treatment, then I would not abhor him. A fool follows the wrong path as if it were the right one, and he tries to persuade his neighbour to follow it also. He gets angry with those who try to teach him and in his self-conceit cannot be helped. Therefore I do not want to see a fool."

The delighted Sakra continued, "Worshipful One! I would like to grant you another boon for these words, which cannot be paid with any price."

So the Bodhisattva, in order to show the King of the Devas that wise people would be agreeable guests to him, said: "May the wise ones come to me and dwell with me and speak to me. Let that be my boon."

"What have the wise ones done for you that you wish to see them?" asked Sakra.

"The Wise-One walks in the path of virtue and leads others on that path also. He has a good education and he accepts what is said to him for his good; therefore I am the friend of the Wise-One."

"As a favovr to me, which I grant out of reverence to you, accept yet another boon," exclaimed the delighted Sakra after these words of the Bodhisattva.

Then the Great One, in order to please Sakra said, "May the food which I have given you and which is full of the practice of charity be given back to me, and may a number of mendicants who are free from bad conduct, come to me to receive it." Sakra said: "Not only shall everything that you have said be accomplished, but on account of your well spoken words you may ask another boon."

Then the Bodhisatta, in order to give the King of the Devas a lesson, said gently: "If you will grant me the highest favour, do not appear to me again in your shining greatness."

Now Sakka became a little irritable and said: "How is it that you, to whom I came

Holy Monks share Ajastyas' food.

without any ritual being performed, without any prayers and vows on your side, as is done by men, who crave for the favour of seeing me—how is it that you, to whom I offer my boons, do not wish to see me ?"

The Bodhisattva said gently: "Do not be angry, King of the Devas, but let me explain myself. Not in irreverence or discourtesy do I ask you not to appear before me again in your glory, but only in order that your shining beauty may not cause me to forget the fulfilment of my religious vows and my penance."

Then Sakra bowed to Him reverently, and, after moving round Him from left to right, he disappeared.

Next morning the Bodhisattva found a great quantity of divine food and drink at the entrance of his hermitage, sent by the power of Sakra, and many holy monks came who had been sent by Sakra and partook of the meal with the Bodhisattva, surrounded by the Devas.

So the Bodhisattva lived on in contentment, a devoted ascetic and divine teacher. Supplied by the Devas daily with divine food and drink, he offered of his bounty, food and teachings to the sages who came to him, till the end of his life, in the Penance-Grove, in the Island of Kara.

XVI.

THE STORY OF UMMÂDAYANTI

Long, long ago, there lived in India a king named Sivikumara. This king who was really the Bodhisattva, was famous on account of his virtues, his wisdom and his liberality. He governed his subjects as a father his children and everybody loved and esteemed him. He set an example of piety to his subjects, and they also loved their religion, and peace and harmony prevailed in the whole empire.

In the capital, where Sivikumara reigned, there lived a very rich man, who had an exceedingly beautiful daughter. She was considered the pearl of womanhood. It was said that she was so beautiful that nobody could look at her without getting bewildered and almost mad and therefore her relatives called her Ummāda-yanti (she who makes mad).

All the rich young men of the town were eager to possess her as their wife, but the father thought that his daughter, being the most beautiful girl in the realm, ought to become the queen. So he went to the king and said to him: "Your Majesty, the goddess of beauty has condescended to enter my house. My daughter is the pearl of all womanhood. Deign to accept her as wife."

So the king sent some Brahmans to the house of the rich man and commanded them to see this beautiful maiden and tell him

Unmâdayanti had to wait on the Brahmans.

whether she would be a suitable queen for him.

The Brahmans came to the house of Ummādayanti's father and the beautiful girl had to wait on her fasher's guests at their meal. But the Brahmans were so overcome with the beauty of the girl, that they could not keep their admiring looks away from her, and the father had to send her away, so that the Brahmans should eat their meal in peace.

When the Brahmans had left the house, where Ummādayanti lived, they consulted with each other and came to the conclusion that the beauty of this girl was enchanting and that it would not be advisable for the king even to see her. They thought that he would surely neglect his religious and political duties and attend only to his lovely Queen, if he married her. And so they reported to the king that the girl was indeed very beautiful, but that she had marks on her, which would bring ruin and ill-luck to the king and so it would be advisable not even to see her.

They said that as the moon, when it is veiled with clouds, hides the beauty of the landscape as well as the brilliancy of the stars, so the veiled beauty of a queen full of charm will hide the good deeds of the king.

And the king, thinking that Ummādayanti had inauspicious marks and was not suitable to be the queen of the land, gave up the idea of seeing her, and her father gave her in marriage to the commander-in-chief of the king's army, Ahipâraka.

But Ummādayanti was not quite satisfied to be the wife of the king's highest subject. She had hoped to become Queen and so she tried and waited an opportunity to be seen by the young king. She thought if only he could see her, then he would become convinced that she, as the most beautiful woman in the whole empire, ought to be Queen.

The opportunity for Ummādayanti of being seen came at last on the occasion of the Kanmudi-festival on the full-moon-night of October-November called then Katika. The whole town was gaily decorated with flags and flowers, the air was filled with the smell of incense and of the sweet flowers which were strewn on the clean white sand of the roads. Gaily dressed people thronged the streets, and singing and dancing were going on everywhere.

Then the king thought he would like to have a look at all this festive decoration in his capital and he ordered his royal chariot to be brought for him. While he was glancing round every where, letting his horses go slowly through the streets, he came to the house of his commander-in-chief Ahipâraka.

There, on the top of the flat roof of this house, stood a woman of surpassing beauty dressed in the daintiest silken cloth, slightly veiled to show the radiance of her beauty even more clearly. She

Report of Brahmans to the King about Unmâdayanti.

The King sees Unmádayanti.

looked at the young king with her brilliant black eyes and the king became quite bewildered and charmed and thought that she must surely be a devi, as mortal woman could hardly be as beautiful as she. He looked back at her again and again and always he saw her eyes turned towards him. "Who could she be?" mused the king. His charioteer said that this house belonged to Ahipâraka and that the beautiful woman on the flat roof was the famous Ummādayanti, who maddened the hearts of the youths who looked at her.

"She is well named" thought the young king, "she has made me almost mad myself. But she is another's wife and I must forget her."

But the young king could not forget her radiant beauty. He recalled her smiles very often and even forgot the regular hours of his kingly duties, which were announced to him, as was the custom at that time when no clocks existed, by the beating on a metal plate every half-hour. Now he had to be roused by the sounding of these gongs to his duty, while before he had seen Ummādayanti, he did not need this reminder; he was always ready for his duties. He tried very hard to forget her, but sleep forsook him and not even dainty food could tempt his appetite. He began to look very ill and the delight in his kingly office had disappeared.

The king's commander-in-chief, who was also his friend, saw the king's grief, and he heard from the charioteer that from the time the king had seen Ummādayanti this change had taken place in him. Ahipâraka asked for an audience with the king and when they were both alone he urged his Majesty to accept his wife Ummādayanti as a gift. The king, not denying that the sight of the beautiful woman had almost maddened him, refused the gift, telling his faithful friehd that he, who had studied the laws, knew that such a thing was very much against them and that he would never think of accepting such a gift when he knew that it would bring grief on his faithful friend and minister.

Although Ahipâraka continued argueing with the king, for he loved him very much, and almost forcing him to agree to the acceptance of this gift, he remained strong, saying that the accepting of his friend's wife as a gift would surely bring unhappiness on the whole kingdom, because it was an evil deed and an unwise example.

"My wife and children are your slaves," answered Ahipâraka "and therefore you do not go against the Law in accepting your slave. It is taught that the one who gives away something dear to him in this world, shall receive his reward in the next, and therefore you will do me a favour in accepting the dearest I have.

The king said: "I am quite sure that you are prompted by the love you bear me, in saying all these things; but your efforts to prove that it would be right for me to accept your gift are not acceptable and I will not neglect righteousness nor will I seek after temporal pleasure at the risk of suffering after death. The virtuous do not seek pleasure at the expense of others."

Still Ahipâraka insisted, thinking of the welfare of the king and wanting to show him his devotion. And the king asked him "Who knows the Law best, the people, you or I?"

":Your Majesty knows best," answered the minister, "because of the labour spent in learning the Law. Your Majesty is the most competent judge in all matters."

"Therefore" answered the king, "you ought not to try to mislead me, for I know that the evil and the good of the people depend on the behaviour of their rulers: and I shall continue above all to tread the path by which I have gained the love of my people. If I should lack the power of ruling my own self, how could I rule my peopie who are looking up to me for protection and for a good example. I look upon my religious duties, and my spotless name for the good of my subjects, and I must lead my people in righteousness and not let my passions lead me."

The minister bowed down in reverence before the great king and said: "Happy the subjects who have such a righteous king, who is a mine of virtue as the sea is a mine of jewels."

And the king overcame his wish to possess the beautiful woman and he reigned on in peace.

XVII.

THE STORY OF THE INHABITANT OF THE BRAHMÁ-LOKA

After many incarnations, the Bodhisattva had acquired so much merit, by the constant practice of Dhyâna,* that he was born in the Brahma-Loka.† But he had not forgotten, in this high state, that in the earth-world there is misery and unhappiness, and he used to look down on earth to find who needed help.

Once as he was thus contemplating the earth, he saw that the King of Vedeha, named Angadiema, was losing himself entirely in the clutches of unbelief, partly in consequence of false convictions and partly because he was led astray by false friends and ministers. He did not believe in life after death, and as he did not know of the law of Karma, (the law of Cause and Effect) he did not care for the

---

*Dhyana Meditation.

† Brahma-Loka—World of the Highest Formless Beings.

The Bodhisattva teaches the king and his followers.

teachings of the Brahmans, but lived a life of sensuality and pleasure.

The Bodhisattva, knowing that the life of the king was looked upon as an example for his people, and would soon demoralise his whole country, decided that he would go down to the earth world and try to help King Angadiema.

So one day, when the king was seated in a lovely arbour in one of his splendid pleasure gardens, the Bodhisattva stood before him in the air, in a shining garment. The king was frightened and bowing down to him with folded hands exclaimed: "Who are you, shining like one of the rays of the sun, using the air as a footstool to your lotus-feet?"

The Bodhisattva answered: "I am one of those Devarshis* of the Brahma-World who have overcome love and hatred."

"Welcome. Oh! High-One," said the king who then washed the feet of the Bodhisattva in humility. "Thou who walkest on the air, as on earth, and whose face shineth like the moon, how didst thou gain this high state?"

"Such power as is mine," answered the Bodhisattva, "is the result of constant meditation, of good conduct and of the control of the senses in former existences."

"Does there really exist another world besides the earth?" asked the king.

---

* Devarshis—Sages among the Devas.

"This truth may be proved by reasoning and by your own senses," answered the Bodhisattva. "Am I not a witness to you about this world higher than the earth ? As well as myself there are people living on earth now, who remember their former existences. Children very often are entirely different from their parents and how can you account for that ? They must have acquired their different characteristics in a former life ! Babes and young animals find the breast of their mother, without being taught. How should they know, if they had not experienced this in a former birth ?

But the king smiled and said : "If thou, oh, great Rishi, wishest me to believe in the next world, lend me five-hundred gold pieces now, and I will return Thee one-thousand in the next world ?"

The Bodhisattva answered : "How could I lend you in this world five-hundred gold pieces to have them returned in the next world with interest ? You, who are a wicked person, will be in hell there. and hell, is so dark and dreadful that I would not go there, where you must suffer in punishment, to ask you for the money, You yourself will not think of the borrowed money there, where reigns only horror and pain. Most likely you will lie on heaps of burning coals, looking like melted gold and you will not think of the borrowed gold, but just moan helplessly. I can give you the description of a thousand more torments, if it will help you to turn your face away from hell."

"Enough, enough," cried the king in alarm, "my mind is full of fear. I have walked on the Path of Evil, having been taught a wrong Doctrine. Be my teacher, my guide, oh thou High One! As the rising sun dispels darkness, so hast thou driven away the darkness of ignorance from me. Lead me in the Path to the Light."

The Bodhisattva pitied the poor King as a father pities his erring son and he saw that he really wanted to lead a better life. He spoke gently to him and the king listened with attention.

"Change thy ways, oh king!" said the Bodhisattva. "Walk on the road to Heaven as other kings nave done before thee. Lead the way for thy subjects to follow. Be virtuous, use thy wealth for the welfare of the poor and thou wilt be happy! Watch thy senses and keep them in restraint, using the bridle of self-restraint upon them as if they were wild horses which have to be tamed. Rule thy subjects as a father his children. Thou art here on earth standing on thy *royal chariot*. Let *worship* of the pious be thy charioteer. Let thine own body giving out virtues, be thy *chariot*. Let *friendliness* be its axle, *self-restraint* and *charity* its wheels and the *earnest desire for gathering merit* be its *spokes*. Restrain thy horses, the organs of thy senses, with that splendid bridle called *attention*. Make *prudence* thy goal and take thy *weapons* from the store of *sacred learning*. Let *shame* be the furniture of thy chariot, *humility* its leading pole, *forbearance* its yoke. Standing on that chariot, thou wilt drive it with skilfulness if thou art firm in courageous self-command.

"Using this vehicle (yâna) brilliant with the lustre of thy *wisdom*, adorned by the flag of thy *good renown* and the high floating banner of thy *tranquility* and followed by *mercy* as its attendants, thou wilt move in the direction of the Highest Goal and never shalt thou descend to the infernal regions, O king."

Thus the Bodhisattva instructed the king, who full of eagerness listened to his teachings. The Bodhisattva, when he saw that the king was a changed man, left him, fully ready to walk on the path of Salvation, and he returned to Brahma-Loka, happy that he had saved the king and his country from destruction.

The king, realizing the teachings of the Bodhisattva, gave from this time such an example to his people that righteousness reigned and the king as well as his people followed the right path to Salvation, believing in a life after death full of either suffering or delight according to one's own doings in this earth-life.

XVIII.

THE STORY OF THE SACRIFICE

It is said in an old Sanskrit manuscript that the Bodhisattva was once born in a high Royal family, and he ascended the throne of his fathers in rightful succession. This high state he had earned by the merit he had acquired in a former birth.

Very often it is, as you know, the case that, when a king is noble-minded and good, the country over which he reigns is good too, or, because the people of the country are good, they have also a good king. Thus it was in this kingdom over which the Bodhisattva ruled as king. There was no strife and there were no epidemics of ilness, and there was peace with all other countries around. The king was almost a Muni in his life, and his good example was followed by all those who surrounded him, and the light of goodness which streamed from the throne, lit up the hearts of his subjects.

Yet once there occurred a calamity which brought a great deal of trouble to the country. Whether the people had done something wrong or whether the Devas in charge of the rain clouds were angry, nobody knew: but a dreadful drought, occurred and all were suffering from the want of water. The wells were dried up and the vegetation was beginning to wither and diseases were threatening in consequence thereof.

The king was afraid that either he or his subjects had neglected some religious duties, and that this drought was the punishment, and so he consulted with his family priest, and the Brahmans and ministers wondered what could be done in this case to put an end to the calamity. The knower of the Vedas said it was necessary, in order to bring down rain, to make a sacrifice of very many animals, because they had read in the Vedas that such sacrifice had produced rain in former times. The king, who was horrified at this suggestion, did not answer but tried to turn the thoughts of his advisers in other directions.

But they were not satisfied and argued: "The king takes care not to neglect his Royal duties. Why is he adverse to make this "sacrifice" which is the bridge to the world of the Devas?"

Then they said to him: "Your Majesty performs the duties to ancestors, to the Rishis and Sages, and to men, but why not to the Devas the duty which is "sacrifice?" Therefore consider the welfare of your subjects and consent to the sacrifice to the Devas of a number of animals, so that we may have rain."

The king thought 'How can the slaughter of animals please the Devas, who are wont to live on ambrosia? Surely such slaughter

The knower of the Vedas proposes the sacrifice to the king.

cannot have any connection with righteousness ! And if the animals are killed while Brahmans are murmuring the prayers, which are to lift them up to heaven *why* do not the Brahmans offer themselves as sacrifice, because *they* want to go to heaven ? The animals are not asked whether they want to be sacrificed and they do not stop their evil ways before they are sacrified, and so how can their death help them to go to heaven ? No, if there are teachings like this, they are wrong. I shall chose another way out of this calamity."

So after these reflections the king said aloud to his counsellors : " Listen to my resolutions. I will not only order an animal sacrifice to be made, but I will offer a human sacrifice as well. Let my officials, in all parts of my country, gather those victims together who are fit to be sacrificed. Let the astrologers find the auspicious day, when the moon and the stars are favourable, and have all other arrangements made for this great sacrifice."

The family priest and the counsellors were amazed, for they had not expected this answer and the priest said, " If the thousand human victims are seized at once, your subjects, your Majesty, will rebel. Therefore take one first, and then gradually the others in succession."

The king replied : " Do not fear the rebellion of my people. Call me together to a meeting of the townspeople and the country-people and I will speak to them myself."

A great meeting was called and the king spoke to the people solemnly: "The drought is great and you have implored me to try my best to end it; therefore I intend to make a great human sacrifice to the Devas.

But nobody who is honest, and charitable and who does not quarrel with his family, or has a faultless character, needs to be afraid that he will be called upon to be sacrificed. I shall send out emissaries, who are honest and far-seeing, into all parts of my country, and they will be known by their dress and they will observe your conduct and they will report to me. Whoever shall be found fault with by these straight-forward watchers will be brought to me for sacrifice. Hear, all ye my subjects, my command!"

And the people went to their homes, rather anxiously, but all bent on doing right, so that they might not be found wanting. The king sent out his officers, and by beat of drum it was proclaimed every day in all towns and villages that the evildoers would be brought to the king to be sacrified, and that their own bad deeds would bring them to the sacrificial spot.

When the people saw the officers of the king walking around everywhere, and heard the same proclamation made every day they all began to mend their ways, quarrels stopped, hospitality was practised everywhere,

By beat of drum it was proclaimed.

good manners and modesty appeared in all places, obedience to parents and teachers in all the houses, and reverence to the gods and to old people. The whole populace of that country lived as if the Kreta-Yuga * had come again. The fear of death had awakened in them all the virtues which they had forgotten before, and in a short time everybody behaved in a splendid way.

But the officers did not relax their watchfulness and the people had to keep up their spotless behaviour.

When the king heard from his officers that they could not find a single evil-doer, he became very glad and gave them rich presents for the good news they brought. And he called his ministers together and said : "There is not a single evil-doer in my country, and I cannot perform the human sacrifice, for the people are so virtuous that they are worthy of receiving sacrifices themselves ; so let me do the sacrifice in my own way. Call the poor and the blind and the lame and give them of my bounty, so that poverty may disappear out of my country."

The ministers had alms-houses erected everywhere and the poor were fed and clothed. Happiness and contentment spread in all directions and the people did not resume their former bad ways and evil deeds ; the plague and all illnesses disappeared. The monsoons brought their regular rains, the wells and rivers

---

* Kreta-Yuga—a former world-period when every body was good.

abounded in pure, clear water, paddy grew abundantly and the medicinal herbs yielded again their healing powers to mankind.

Thus, by the power of the good king and the greatness of the sacrifice which he performed in his own way, the country was saved from all troubles, and the people lived in happiness and contentment, blessing their saintly king for all he had done for them, and not forgetting that, if they were to begin evil ways again, they would be seized and used as a human sacrifice, as their king had announced so many times.

In the meanwhile the king, who had proclaimed that this sacrifice was to be made, had put aside his kingly robes and wore a black deer skin as his garb, and putting his royal umbrella and crown aside, wore his hair in the manner prescribed by the Vedas for those who perform a great sacrifice. Thus he lived and died, and his subjects adored him almost as a god.

His example induced other kings also to reform and be more considerate to their subjects, for the renown of the saintly king, his contentment and the happiness of his subjects spread far and wide over the whole Eastern world.

Pure-heartedness, wisdom and righteousness are illustrated in this story of one of the lives of the Bodhisattva, who was working up his way to perfection, to become the "Buddha," the Saviour of his people.

XIX.

THE STORY OF SAKRA

It is said that, after the Bodhisattva had already practised meritorious deeds for a long, long time, his splendid Karma brought him birth in the Deva-kingdom, and he became the king of the Devas.

With the Bodhisattva as Sakra, the magnificence of the Deva-kingdom was greater than ever. It shone like a palace, just renewed in all its splendour, whose beauty is enhanced by the beams of the full-moon falling on it. But Sakra was not proud of his greatness, nor of that of his kingdom. He ruled heaven and earth in his usual spirit of righteousness, justice and compassion, and the might of the Deva-kingdom surpassed everything.

But the Daityas or Asuras* became very jealous, and could not stand seeing this bliss and happiness, so they renewed their war against the Devas, which they had ceased for some centuries. They marched against the Devas with a mighty army of elephants, chariots, and horses, and they caused such dreadful noises to arise that they sounded like the ocean, when its waves are lashed by a furious storm. The Demons carried so many weapons that one could hardly see the fighters themselves behind them.

---

* Demons of the darkness. Their war with the Devas (or gods of light) is eternal and a common topic in Indian mythology (Prof. Spencer's note.)

Thus Sakra, although opposed to war, in his life of righteousness and compassion, had to stand againt the forces of the Daityas, so as to defend his kingdom. He mounted his golden chariot, which was blazing with jewels and which had on its banner a figure clad in the robes of an Arhat. It was drawn by a thousand white horses. So, surrounded by his host of warriors, he met the army of the Daityas just on the border-line of the Great Ocean Here a fierce battle was fought, which almost equalled the destruction of a world. The chariots rolled over the battle-field, as the thunder rolls over the heavens, and the clash of the weapons, meeting in combat, flashed like lightnings.

At last the army of Sakra took flight, overcome by the fierce attack of the fiery weapons of the Demons. Only Sakra himself stood firm in his chariot with its one thousand horses, barring the way of the demons.

Then Mâtali, the charioteer of the King of the Devas, seeing the army of the Daityas which he feared would overcome the chariot, thought it was time to retreat, and the thousand horses were guided towards the ascent to heaven. But while doing so, the Lord of the Devas saw in a tall cotton tree the nest of some eagles, containing some young birds, not old enough to make their escape by flight. So he called out to his charioteer to take care that these nests were not destroyed by the pole of the chariot, which was pointed just in that direction.

"I cannot avoid destroying these birds" answered the charioteer, "as the Demons are close behind us, and if I take another direction, they will overcome us."

"Never mind the Demons," answered the Lord of the Devas, "save the nests of the young eagles!" "Only by stopping the chariot, can I save the nests," answered Mâtali, "and then the Demons will have the better of the Devas."

Thus Sakra, moved by compassion for the birds, said: "Stop the chariot, I would rather die by the clubs of the enemies than destroy the lives of these helpless birds, which are loudly screaming to me for pity." The chariot stood still with its thousand horses and the Daityas were amazed to see this heroism. When they saw that the Lord of the Devas was ready to fight single-handed the whole army of the Demons, they became so confused and frightened that, instead of attacking the Lord of the Devas, their ranks gave way, and, as a wind drives away the rain-clouds, so they were dispersed in flight by terror.

The Devas, seeing this, returned and it was an easy task for them to follow up the Demons, who could not gather together their ranks.

So once more the Daityas were conquered and peace reigned in the land of the Devas as long as the Bodhisattva was their Lord.

Such was the life of the Bodhisattva, when he was the Lord of the Devas, and so he protected even then the lives of the birds, who appealed to him for mercy, exposing his own life to the attack of the whole army of the Demons. The Demons took fright on account of His goodness and they could not harm Him. He had conquered the whole army of the Evil Ones with one compassionate look.

XX.

THE STORY OF THE BRAHMAN

In this story we see the Bodhisattva as the son of a Brahman family wao had a great reputation for goodness and charity. All the members of the family were learned and they kept closely to the Brahminical customs.

When the Bodhisattva was old enough to receive the teachings of the Vedas, he was sent with other Brahman youths to a celebrated teacher (Guru) and he lived with him in his very poor home.

The Bodhisattva was so exceptionally clever, well-behaved and devoted to his studies, that his Guru took a great pleasure in teaching him and became very much attached to him.

In order to test his pupils, the Guru began to complain of his utter poverty and of the simple food, which was brought to him by his pupils. So his disciples tried to bring their teacher the best food they could collect by begging, as it was against the

The Guru in his hermitage.

custom to bring any other food but what was given in charity, and they themselves had to eat it also, so long as they were under the roof of the Brahman, who had to live on gifts.

The Guru was even then not satisfied and constantly complained of his poverty and he said to them: "Do not exert yourselves with trying to bring me better food: it does not help my poverty as it is given as alms. The pain which poverty brings can only be destroyed by wealth, as food destroys hunger, and medicine disease."

"If we could beg for wealth," answered the pupils, "we would surely not let our beloved teacher suffer like this. But, as Brahmans can only gain wealth by the receiving of gifts and nobody will give us riches, we are powerless and do not know how to relieve your sufferings."

The Brahman replied: "But there *are* other means of earning money, and these means are even explained in the law-books. I am now old and infirm, I am not able to use these means."

"But, *we* are not old and infirm," said the pupils; "show us the way to earn this wealth for you, and we will follow your teachings." The teacher answered. "I am afraid your minds are not strong enough to follow out these teachings; but still I will tell you what to do. It is written in the law-books, that in *time of distress, theft* is allowable for the Brahmans, who in fact are the owners of the whole world. *Poverty* seems to me the greatest distress in the world and therefore your taking of things for me in my great poverty will not be wrong, if you do it in a lonely place, without getting caught or losing your reputation."

The pupils were astonished at such teachings, but they thought (finding perhaps an echo in their own hearts in favour of this unsound argument), that they would follow his suggestions, and they all departed in search of wealth.

Only one pupil remained silent, and with a deep sigh he turned away from his Guru withou approval, and this was the Bodhisattva. "How is it, that you alone disapprove of my advice as to how to gain riches?" asked the Brahman. "Are you not strong and courageous enough to do what your fellow students will do for me, or is your love for me not as great as theirs? Does not my sorrow touch your heart"?

The Bodhisattva bowed low before his Guru and said: "It is not want of love for you, my Guru, nor want of courage, but I think that the way of gaining riches, of which you speak, is wrong. For me there is no lonely spot where I could do an evil action. Do not the Devas and Munis see what we are doing, and, even if they were not watching us, is not our own Self there to see our evil deeds? No! my revered Guru, I cannot go with my fellow-students to commit theft, even if it be done to help you in your poverty" "Besides," continued the Bodhisattva, after being encouraged by his teacher to speak on, "I cannot believe that my beloved Guru means to teach

Food-Supplies.

us that wrong is right, knowing the difference between virtue and vice. It is better to be satisfied with the offerings of the people in food and clothing, mean though they may be, than to murder righteousness even if the goal were to reach the heaven of the Devas."

Overjoyed by the words of his disciple, the old Brahman got up from his seat, embracing his disciple very affectionately and saying: "You alone of all my disciples have understood my test. You alone understand the Scriptures and know that the greatest wealth is "wisdom." My teaching has not been fruitless, as there is one who fully understands me. You, the spotless one of your pure family, understood the Law and will become the Teacher of the Law."

So the Bodhisattva stood alone, among his fellow-students, like the sun that shines, lonely, but majestically, obscuring in daytime all the other heavenly bodies by its light of purity and strength.

XXI.

THE STORY OF THE JAR

In the course of his lives advancing towards Buddhahood, the Bodhisattva was again the King of the Devas, Sakra. He had all he wanted and could enjoy all the happiness and splendour of the Deva-kingdom, but his heart was set on relieving pain or in teaching the Devas as well as hnman beings.

One day the Bodhisattva, the Deva-king, was casting his benevolent eye over the world, to see what he could do to better mankind. Looking over India's wide realm he saw a king whose name was Sarvamitra (which means everybody's friend) originally a very good and kind-hearted man, who had fallen into the habit of drinking, led by his unscrupulous ministers and friends. Sarvamitra did not see anything wrong in drinking and so his people followed his bad example and drinking and revelling were the habits of all the people in his kingdom.

"What can I do to show this good king how wrong it is to follow this Path of Destruction, which looks at first very fair and smooth, but which ends in an abyss." thought Sakra "I must cure the king, for, if he is not cured of the drinking habit, his subjects will follow his example, and the destruction, which is awaiting the whole country, will not be averted."

So the Bodhisattva, in the shape of a Brahman, with bark garment and deer-skin, appeared in the air before the king and his drinking companions one day, when they were just discussing the merits of several different intoxicants. The Brahman before them in the air looked so formidable, but so good, that the king and his followers got up from their seats and bowed to him reverently, taking him, perhaps, for some god.

Sakra explains the contents of the Jar.

The Brahman standing now in their midst, spoke with a loud voice, resembling the rain falling heavily from a thunder-cloud : "See, oh King, I have here a jar brim-full, adorned with laughing flowers, as if shaken by the low breath of the wind. See how proud it looks. Will you buy it from me ? "

The king was full of curiosity who this remarkable looking being might be, and what were the contents of the jar, which was hanging down from his left side, So he folded his hands in reverence and looked up to him and spoke : " You have come to us like the morning sun in glory and like the moon in gracefulness. Your figure inspires awe like some Muni's. What is your name and who are you ? "

" Who I am, I will tell you later on," answered the Bodhisattva : " first I want you to buy this jar from me ; that is, if you are not afraid to purchase with it suffering in this world and in the next."

The king looked very much astonished and answered : " Generally wares for sale are praised and their faults are hidden. You speak of suffering, which follows the purchase of your jar. Verily you must be one of those Brahmans, who always speak the truth, as was the custom of the twice-born. Tell me then, oh Truthful One, what this jar contains, and what would be its equal in value to you."

Sakra answered : " The jar does not contain holy water, nor honey gathered from the sweetest flowers, nor butter, nor milk with the colour of moonbeams, awaking the water-lilies on a cloudless night! This jar contains strong vicious liquor. And now I will explain to you the properties of this liquor."

"The one who drinks this "*surâ*" loses power over his mind as well as over his body. His enemies laugh at him, because he behaves like a beast. This bright liquor in this jar affects men and women the same way, so that even the timid and bashful, after drinking from it, lose all their timidity. This liquor turns friends into enemies so that they kill each other in their fury. This "*surâ*" brings ruin and destruction to wealthy and noble families; it makes the tongue loose and the limbs tremulous, the eyes dull and heavy and it ruins the mind and makes a man contemptible to every one. Even old people are affected by the drinking of this liquor, so that they cannot follow the path of righteousness. A curse lies in this golden-coloured fluid which makes the drinker speak falsehood, as if it were Truth, and commit evil deeds as if they were right. Buy this drink which causes madness, oh king! this mother of sins, so that without caring for the future state or for happiness you may do what you like. This beverage, called *surâ* deprives man of virtue, and becoming accustomed to the drinking of it. men become beasts or behave like pretas (ghosts). They are walking on the path of Avicci, which, though at first smooth and broad, ends in destruction."

"In short, by drinking this *surâ*, oh king, exery virtue is destroyed!

"Can you, after hearing all this go on drinking this vile destroyer of all happiness?"

The king was touched by the words of Sakra, spoken as a father to his son, or as an Arhat to his disciple, and he saw with his mind's eye the consequences of the use of this sin producing liquor.

He cast the desire for it away at once and throwing himself down before Sakra said: "You have spoken like a father to me and your well spoken words have shown me your wisdom and your goodness. Deign to accept from me a gift as well as my worship. Five good villages, a hundred slaves, five hundred cows, ten chariots with the best horses to draw them, I give to you, my Gūru for the words you have spoken. Or if you wish for something else it will be at your disposal."

Sakra answered: "I do not want villages, slaves, cows or chariots. I am Sakra the King of the Devas. All these things are mine already. You call me a speaker of wise words! The speaker of wise words wants to be honoured by the acceptance of these words and by their being acted upon. Give up the habit of drinking, oh king with the good heart! and you will walk on the Path of Righteousness and guide your subjects on the road which leads to salvation."

Saying this, Sakra disappeared. The king, remembering the words of the Bodhisattva, at once stamped out in himself the desire for drink, and his subjects following his example, became thrifty and content and from that day the appearance of the whole country was changed.

And so also you, who are inclined to the evil habit of drinking, take heed of the words of the Bodhisattva in the shape of Sakra, who convinced King Sarvamitra that drink is the mother of all evil.

"I abstain from taking intoxicating liquor"

XXII.

THE STORY OF AVISHAHYA.

It was the good Karma of a rich merchant in India that this time the Bodhisattvs should be born as his son, and should follow in his footsteps, becoming in his turn not only a merchant, but the head of the Guild of Merchants. He had received an excellent education, had a clear insight into all affairs, but withal was liberal and practised charity in the widest sense of the word. His wealth became so great, that he was called the king of merchants, and by the strength of his character he walked firmly on the path of charity, from which no vice or temptation of any kind could lure him: hence was he named "Avishahya," which means the "Invincible One."

Now, beggars continually crowded round him, eaeh of whom he considered as his guest, and whatever were their wishes. he denied them nothing. His face as well as those of his poor friends bsamed happily when they departed. He was not at all attached to his riches, and he rejoiced when the mendicants carried away the best things out of his house. To him, his wealth was only a means by which he could accomplish good deeds and no monk or beggar left his house without being perfectly satisfied with the gifts of the charitable Avishahya. When Sakra, the King of the Devas, heard of the wonderful charity of Avishahya, he was amazed, and wished to try how far the love of almsgiving would go with the rich merchant, so he made the gifts of provisions, grains, money and clothes, which Avishahya had got ready for distribution, disappear every day. Avishahya wondered what had become of the things, but he sent every time for fresh supplies, and the poor always left him happy and satisfied. He himself, although his wealth dwindled awao, became more satfsfied every day.

Sakra was more amazed than ever when he saw that Avishahya ceased not from his bountiful almsgiving, so he resolved to make the charitable merchant quite poor in one night, and he wondered whether *that* would stop his desire for helping others.

One morning, when Avishahya awoke early he found his house quite empty. Neither, furniture, nor clothes, nor provisions, nor money were to be found, and even his dttendants had disappeared. His house looked as if it had been plundered by Rakshasas. He searched everywhere, but he found only a coil of rope in one corner, and in another a sickle.

Avishahya wondered, and then said aloud "Who can have taken my things away? Is it someone who, not used to begging, has taken them because he is accustomed to get his livelihood by his own energy? Then my wealth is well spent!"

"Or has somebody taken them whom my high rank has made envious"? In this case it would be a pity, for the things would be of no use to anybody. What shall I do when the poor people come to my empty house, and I cannot feed or clothe them? They are accustomed to receive gifts and hospitality from me, and now, behold! my house is like a dried-up pond where the thirsty cannot find water to drink."

Nevertheles, the Bodhisattva, not able to beg himself, as he was always wont to give, found out in his present state of poverty how hard it must be for those who had to beg, and his compassion for the beggars became greater. In order to make it possible to give, if even in a very small way, he took the rope and the sickle, the only possessions remaining to him, and and went out to cut grass day after day. From the sale of this grass, he first gave food to the beggars, and then took enough to keep himself from starving. In this way he lived for some time, happy that he could give, and satisfy the hunger of some

The coils of rope and the sickle left to Avishahya.

sick and aged people, who could not help themselves.

But Sakra, seeing that even great poverty could not shake Avishahya in his devotion to almsgiving, was filled with admiration. Showing himself to the Bodhisattva in his celestial body and standing in the air before him he said, trying him still further : "Householder, thieves have not robbed you of your wealth, neither have water nor fire done so, nor envious princes; you alone have brought this condition of poverty on yourself. Therefore renounce that passionate love of charity. If in your present poverty you begin to accumulate the little you earn, you will have riches again at last, even as anthills grow because the ants gather soil together little by little."

The Bodhisattva was not convinced by Sakra's argument but answered : "No gentleman, however unhappy he may be, will do anything ignoble. I would never wish to gather riches if I could do it only by becoming a miser. I could never accept any jewels or wealth, or even heaven, if I were not allowed to use them for gladdening the hearts of the poor ones. If receiving increases the vice of selfishness, then I must do away with it entirely, for in that case it is evil. Wealth comes and goes like a flash of lightning, but charity brings constant happiness."

"Householder," Sakra answered : "What thou sayest suits a wealthy man, but thou hast no riches. If thou dost again heap up riches, then, if thou wouldst give some of them away, nobody would blame thee. But the one who has the love for charity without the means of gratifying it, is like a bird that wants to fly before his wings are grown. What meanness could there be in giving up the longing for charity if there were no ways for giving?"

The Bodhisattva replied: "Every person ought to be charitable, for there does not exist any gladness which equals that which comes through charitable deeds. Besides, riches without charity cannot lead to heaven. Neither can riches subdue selfishness or other vices. He who, moved by compassion, is willing to give away even his very self in order to protect the old and poor and sick, enjoys bliss everlasting. Once a carriage has made a track on the road a second one can follow out more easily. I have driven this first carriage, when I was rich; now I have confidence to drive over the same track again as it is easier, and I shall not leave the right track. If I should get wealth again, it certainly shall be given to the needy ones. Till then I shall give the little I can."

Sakra marvelled at hearing the words of the Bodhisattva and looking at him with awe he said: "Others grasp at riches and do not fear even dangers in getting them, but they are attached to them in order to gain pleasure Thou dost not even pine at the loss of the riches nor at my temptation, but thy mind is set on promoting the welfare of others. Oh, thy heart shines out like a light set in a dark place. Thou sufferest by the loss of thy wealth only because, moved by thy heartfelt compassion, thou canst not help others as well as thou couldst before. I see I have not shaken thee by my temptation more than a mountain covered with snow is shaken by the wind. It was I who had hidden thy wealth from thee in order to make thy fame greater by trial, even as gold is refined by fire. So, Great-One, pour out thy wealth as a cloud pours its rain into the dry ponds and wells. By my favour thou shalt never lose thy wealth any more and I pray thee to forgive me for trying and tempting thee."

After saying this the king of the Devas disappeared, having been granted pardon by the Bodhisattva for his manner of testing him.

Great wealth came back to Avishahya and his house was filled again with the poor and the afflicted, who never left except with happy faces and grateful hearts. The wealth of the charitable merchant never failed and till his death he was the father of the poor

---

This story teaches us that the really virtuous person is never wanting in charity; and even in danger and peril and poverty he will find means to assist those who n
help.

XXIII.

THE STORY OF CUDDABODHI

The following story shows that, by keeping down anger, a person can subdue those who want to do him harm.

Once the Bodhisattva was born as the son of a noble Brahman, who had a great reputation as a virtuous and liberal man. He educated his son in all the necessary arts and sciences, and soon Cuddabodhi (as he was called) became famous in the assemblies of the Wise Ones. He became known as *the jewel* among all the jewels, or as *the hero* among the heroes.

He studied the Dharma arduously, and when he became aware of his former existences and of his former acquaintance with the Law, the house in which he dwelt seemed to him too small. He felt that he wanted to renounce the world and go into the forest as a wandering ascetic. When his wife heard this, (he was living at the time as a householder and he had a good and lovely wife), she made up her mind to follow him into the forest. When he cut off his hair and put on the garments of an ascetic, she also cut off her beautiful long hair, took off all her jewels and her silk sari and put on the yellow robe of an ascetic.

Cuddabodhi told her that the life of a homeless ascetic was too hard a life for her and that, if she wanted to renounce the world, she should go to a place where other women were living, who likewise had renounced the world. But the devoted woman would not listen to Cuddabodhi and she followed him at a distance. Whenever he rested under a tree or in an empty shed, she rested not far from him, but she did not trouble him by talking to him or disturb him in his meditations. So they wandered through villages and towns and at last they came into a forest. Here the Bodhisattva sat down under a large tree to go into deep meditation. It was a beautiful forest in which they were. The trees stood together in groves so close that the sun could only peep through the dense foliage. The petals of the wood-flowers were strewn on the ground like a carpet, and no noise of the outer world reached there. It was just the right place for meditation.

The devoted woman also sat down under a tree and her thoughts too dwelt on the bliss of renunciation. Busy bees hummed round her and the happy cries of the cuckoo sounded everywhere. Water lilies and lotuses smiled at her feet in the pool close by, and soft winds fanned her cheeks. She herself 'looked like a goddess of beauty in all the loveliness around her.

Just that thought of beauty filled the heart of the king of that country, who, wanting to enjoy the delights of a spring-day in the forest, came in his wanderings to the tree where the follower of Cuddabodhi sat in all her beauty, clad only in the yellow dress of an ascetic. Then the king noticed the Bodhisattva not far from her under another tree, joining some rags together for cloth after having finished his meditation. The king bowed before him and said: "Ascetic, there are rogues everywhere in this world, it is not right of you to have such a handsome companion with you when you are without pretection yourself, What could you do if somebody should injure her? You could only cry in rage and that would disturb the quiet of your religious life, Therefore let her live in an inhabited place. What use is the company of a woman for an ascetic?"

"You have spoken the truth O king," said the Bodhisattva, "but whoever would injure her would be haunted by me as a thunder cloud ready to break at any moment."

The king thought: "This ascetic takes an interest in that woman, but he has not reached the state where he has gained miraculous powers by his penance." So, not being afraid of evil doing, the king ordered his attendants to seize the handsome woman, and put her in one of his chariots to take her to his palace.

The poor woman began to cry and she spoke through her tears: "One ought to look upon the king as a protector, and father, but to whom can one look, when the king himself does wrong? Are the guardians of the world's quarters asleep, or do they not exist, that they do not protect the suffering? But why call on the gods, when my master and Lord

The King carries away the Bodhisattva's wife.

himself is quiet and does not care as to my fate? Must I, wretched woman, see this indifference, when a single curse would destroy this king? Ought not an ascetic to have compassion on any person in distress?"

Thus the poor woman cried and wailed; but the Bodhisattva arranging his rags quietly, apparently did not seem to take any heed of his wife being put into the king's chariot to be carried away by force.

The king wondered at this and turning to the Bodhisattva he said: "At first you threatened the one who should injure the woman, your companion, and now, when I am taking her away by force, you are quiet because you have no power to help her. Why not show your power by a miracle and save her?"

"I have shown my power by subduing the one who struggled against me", answered the Bodhisattva firmly and quietly.

"I do not understand you," said the king: Whom have you subdued?"

"Listen" said the Bodhisattva: "The dust is subdued by the rain: anger is the giant whom I conquered, anger who robs man of his insight and of his forbearance: anger, at whose appearance the enemy rejoices, rose up in me and I conquered him: anger, who stirs up in a person all evil and who overcomes all good gained by penance; who destroys like fire the one in whom it is kindled. He who cannot appease the heart-burning fever of anger loses his reputation like the moonbeams that fade away from the waterlilies at the break of day. A man overcome with anger misses the road to salvation. He plunges himself into the blinding dust of passion and he cannot distinguish right from wrong. Anger was struggling in me, but I did not release him for I know he is an enemy, who does so much mischief. And, therefore, I struggled with anger till I conquered him."

These words spoken by the Bodhisattva struck the king with astonishment and admiration: "The words you have spoken to me," he said, "are worthy of your great mind. Pardon me, as I did not understand the meaning of your tranquility."

And throwing himself down before the Bodhisattva, the king confessed his sins to him, asked his forgiveness and offered his services to him. He also released the weeping woman after asking for her pardon.

Anger does not cease by anger.
Anger only ceases by love.

XXIV.

THE STORY OF SUTASOMA

Once, it is said, the Bodhisattva was born in the famous family of the Kauravas in India. His father the king was very virtuous, and his subjects worshipped him on account of his justice and power. He lived in peace with the neighbouring kings, whom he had reduced to a state of vassalage. The king's son was called Sutasoma, which means 'Lovely as the Moon-God Soma,' because he was beautiful to look upon.

He grew up in virtue and he was very fond of learning, so that Sutasoma became even more famous than his father, and it was said that he possessed the sixteen virtues corresponding to the sixteen phases of the moon*; such for instance as, good conduct, learning, charity, mercy, self-command patience, humility and so on.

So the old king declared him heir-apparent, and made him take half the responsibilities of the throne upon himself.

The kingdom was now well governed and the people lived in unity, contentment and happiness, following the example of the king and his royal son Sutasoma.

Sutasoma, because of his love for religion, used to encourage the Brahmanas in bringing

---

* In India, astronomers divide the disc of the moon into 16 parts.

to him learned moral stanzas for which, if he was satisfied with them, he paid very liberally. He was also a lover of nature, and many a time he wandered about in the forests surrounding his capital.

Once, in the month of flowers, the lovely month of May, nature had donned her most lovely and fragrant apparel and the trees and bushes laughed brightly in their brilliancy of flowers. The deep blue lakes in the forest were covered with the varied coloured flower petals, fallen from the overhanging trees. The busy humming of the industrious bees, gathering honey from the blossoms, sounded in the air, and balmy breezes, rendered fragrant by the breath of the flowers, swayed the branches of the trees, which sheltered the little brightly feathered birds. So beautiful was the forest that Sutasoma felt the need of roaming about in it. He called his wives and their guards, his own body-guard and some of his warriors and with the whole suite went out into the woods. Merry laughter and the melodious songs of the queens and royal maidens filled the air, and the happy faces and gay draperies of all these beautiful women made the scene a very attractive one.

Sutasoma, more spectator than actor, was seated under a shady tree, when a Brahman approached him, saying that he had brought some remarkable stanzas, which he begged permission to read to the prince. The prince, well pleased, granted the request, for, in spite of all the sounds of rejoicing, his mind was ever open to teachings: So he settled himself down to listen quietly to the wise thoughts of the Brahman.

All at once, all merriment ceased, and confused cries coming from the forest side where the guards were stationed, announced the presence of some trouble. One of the warriors came running to him with a frightened face, crying: "Your majesty, a great misfortune threatens us—Kalmashapada, the son of Sudāsa, the man-eater approaches you: He has dispersed your warriors, has even driven away your elephants, and frightened the chariot horses."

"Who is this man you call a man-eater?" asked Sutasoma (although he knew very well what this meant).

"Is it possible that your majesty does not know the story of this Kalmashapada, the son of a lioness and the adopted son of the king Sudasa?"

"Why is he called the man-eater?" asked the prince.

Then the trembling warrior replied: "In a word, a strong boy, the son of a lioness was found by the forester, who took him to King Sudasa who being childless, adopted the boy. When the king Sudāsa died, this boy became king. All went well until, having once tasted human flesh, he grew so fond of it that, to obtain it, he had the prisoners killed, and ate their bodies. When they were all devoured, he actually had some of his subjects put to death for the same purpose so that his people resolved to destroy him."

"Then the son of Sudasa made a pact with the Rakshashas, who are eaters of human flesh, promising to sacrifice to them a hundred princes, if they would save him from the threatened danger of being killed by his subjects. The Rakshashas saved him and he now lives in a ruin in this forest, where he has carried off many a royal prince, and he is coming to carry off your majesty also. Now that you have heard the story, deign to give us your orders O Prince!"

Sutasoma answered: "A man who has lost his humanity is like a madman and deserves pity beyond anything else. Weapons are of no avail in this instance, I will try to destroy his wickedness. Therefore it is enough for all of you to do your ordinary duties."

He comforted those around him, and told them that he would offer the man-eater hospitality if he came near him, and with these words, Sutasoma went in the direction of the noise he heard and found his soldiers in confusion, pursued by a wild looking giant. His soiled garments hung loosely around him, his face was almost hidden by a thick black beard, while on his head he wore a crown of bark and leaves. In his hands were a sword and a shield.

The Prince carried away by Sandâsa's son.

Sulasoma preaches to Sandâsa's son.

Sutasoma stepped forward without fear, and weaponless, called out, "Here I am, turn on me and do not trouble these poor people."

The son of Sudasa turned round, and seeing the prince standing there alone and unarmed pounced upon him like a lion on his prey, seized him and placing him on his shoulders ran off with him saying:

"You are the very man I was seeking."

Thus he entered his strongnold, carrying Sutasoma. The place looked worse than a cemetery. Corpses lay around, fresh blood moistened the ground, and the smoke of many funeral pyres darkened the trees which grew near by.

Amongst these horrors, the son of Sudasa put the prince down and stared at him, wondering at his beauty and gentleness.

The prince was thinking of the Brahman who had come to the park just before he had been carried away by this monster, and, regretting not having heard his stanzas and wondering what the Brahman would think of his not coming back, a sigh broke from his lips and a tear gathered in his eye.

The son of Sudasa seeing this, laughed aloud and said. "I see that all your renowned wisdom does not prevent your sorrow at finding yourself now in my power. Do you grieve for life or wealth, or for pleasure, for your rank, your parents or wives or children? Tell me the truth, why do you weep?"

The Bodhisattva answered:

"I do not grieve about myself or my relatives, but because, just before you carried me away, a Brahman had come, bringing me some wise stanzas, and he is now disappointed at not receiving the reward I am accustomed to give to those who teach me Only give me leave to hear those sweet words of wisdom and I will come back to you, and you may then do with me what you will."

"What you say," answered the son of Sudāsa. "is astonishing. He who has gazed into the eyes of Death, has been held by him, and then has been released, would never return to him of his own free will. What motive would induce him to return?"

"Do you not understand the motive that would bring me back to you?" asked the prince. "Have I not *promised* to come back. I am not a villain, I am Sutasoma, and my word is my bond. It is true that some 'through fear of death' might forget their promise; but those do not tread the path of virtue. Have you seen anything in me that causes you to suspect me? Did I not meet you without fear and unarmed? Persons like myself do not tell an untruth! So let me go to hear the stanzas of the Brahman, and I shall return to you at once."

The son of Sudāsa was very much astonished at the words of the Bodhisattva but, as he was curious to see whether the prince really would return, and as he did not care so much to retain him, having already captured the hundred princes whose sacrifice he had promised to the Rakshasas he said :

"Well go then and attend to your Brahman, and return to me. I shall thus have time to prepare your funeral pyre. I really wonder whether you will be faithful and keep your pledge."

So the Bodhisattva returned to the palace, to the great joy of all there. He sent for the Brahman, who delighted him by four stanzas full of advice and virtue. After having rewarded him most generously, he went to the king and told him that he was obliged to resign his kingly office, as he had promised the son of Sudāsa to return to him, after having heard the words of advice of the Brahman.

"Surely" cried the old king in alarm "you will not keep your promise to that horrible man-eater? I cannot allow you to return to him. There is no sin in breaking a promise made to a man, who does not even know what it is to be truthful. You, as future king, must act politically, in this exceptional case, to protect your person by not following too strictly the path of Righteousness. Besides, you should consider the grief of your father and family. But if you do not agree to this and insist on keeping your promise, then return to that monster, surrounded by your mighty army, your elephants, horses and chariots, and either subdue or kill him. In that way you will have fulfilled your promise of return.

"No," my father, answered Sutasoma, "I cannot promise one thing and do another; besides, this man-eater deserves my pity, being enslaved by evil habits, and making his own road to hell. He has acted very generously to me in releasing me after capturing me, only relying on my promise to return. I must keep that promise, my father, and besides I am confident that he will not injure me."

So at last the king let him go. He went alone, in spite of all the entreaties of his friends and his warriors, who were very anxious to protect him.

When the son of Sudāsa saw prince Sutasoma approaching his strong-hold quite alone and unarmed he was so amazed that he could hardly, believe his eyes, and he exclaimed:

"But this is wonderful. Is it possible that he carries truth to this extreme, coming back to such a cruel person as I am? Surely his renown as a truth-speaker is well deserved as I see for myself!"

The Bodhisattva approached and said:

"I have obtained the treasure of these holy teachings from the Brahman and my mind has been gladdened, thanks to you. I have rewarded the Brahman, and now I have come back to you, according to my word. Eat me, if you so desire, or sacrifice me to the Rakshashas. I am ready."

"I am not in a hurry to devour you," said the man-eater, "the funeral-pyre is yet smoking, and human flesh tastes best when roasted by a smokeless fire." So repeat first to me the holy verses, which pleased you so much."

"What use can holy verses, be to you?" asked the Bodhisattva "You have left the "Path of Righteousness to follow the Path of Evil. You love injustice and hate righteousness, you only live to satisfy the cravings of your stomach, you live like a Rakshasha, so these holy sayings are not for you."

"Do not condemn me altogether," exclaimed the man-eater, "hunters shoot the innocent deer, whilst I only shoot men. The hunters are not blamed—whilst I am called evil."

"Those who kill animals do not walk on the Path of Righteousness," said the Bodhisattva, "but you, a man-eater, are very much more evil, for man takes by his birth the highest place of all, and he is not meant for food."

The son of Sudāsa, although vexed at this reproach, answered with a laugh.

"You have shown me, by coming back to me here after I released you, that you do not understand political wisdom at all, having acted quite against its principles."

"On the contrary" answered the prince "I am well skilled in political wisdom, but in this case I did not practise it, because I should have had to act against righteousness and break my faith with you, by attending to the preservation of my body."

"Of what use is this truth of which you think so highly?" asked the son of Sudāsa.

"Truth brings merit, and it is more effectual than penance. Truth is the entrance-door to Nirvana, and the bridge of safety over the swamps of Samsāra."

The son of Sudāsa looked at the prince with an admiring but bewildered glance and said:

"When other men are in my power, they are paralysed by fear and all their courage goes. Do you not fear death at all?"

"Why should I fear death?" answered the Bodhisattva, "which is an unavoidable thing. Only those fear death who are afraid of suffering in the other world, because of having done evil deeds in this one. Only their bad conscience causes them to fear death. I do not remember ever having done anything bad, therefore why should I fear death? Even after thinking for a long time, I cannot remember ever having had an evil thought, so that, when I see the way to Nirvana thrown open to me, I have no fear. I have built many alms-houses, hermitages and tanks, and, as I have helped wherever I could, why should I be afraid of death? I am ready to be eaten by you!"

The darkness of wickedness cleared from the eyes of the man-eater, and with tears filling his eyes he exclaimed:

"Surely, not even the vilest person could do evil to such a holy man as you are. I see the ugliness of my conduct in the mirror of Righteousness; may you have mercy on me and teach me the Law."

The Bodhisattva saw that he was eager to learn and so he answered gently: "Those who wish for the teachings of the Law must show their gentleness by taking a lower seat than that of their Teacher, and they must listen to the teacher of the Law, even as a sick man listens to the advice of his doctor."

Then the son of Sudāsa took off his upper garment, and, laying it upon a stone, invited the Bodhisattva to be seated, while he himself sat at his feet up the ground.

Then the Bodhisattva began thus:

"Hear these stanzas, which I learned from the Brahman after you released me from my captivity. Because of your generosity towards me, I have had the happiness of acquiring them, and you shall share my happiness.

'Meet but once a virtuous man, it will suffice to form a lasting friendship, depending not on further meeting."'

"That is true," called out the listening man-eater, "go on! go on!"

'"From the virtuous keep not thyself remote. But follow, and to worship them, thyself devote. He who approaches them cannot fail to become like them."'

"Such persons are like the flower dust, giving forth unknowingly the sweet perfume of noble words and deeds."

"Go on! go on" cried the son of Sudāsa, eagerly.

'"The ears of kings, with jewels and with gold
Lose with the jewels their beauty, growing old!
So strong a love of virtue, pious men possess
That never does it fade, but lives to bless.
And distant as the East is from the West
As distant as the earth from Heaven's throng
And Ocean's shores however wide apart,
Still greater is the space 'twixt Right and Wrong."'

"Lovely are the Gathas I have heard!" cried the son of Sudāsa. "You have given me joy in the recitation of them, so accept from me in return, four boons."

"How can you grant boons?" cried the Bodhisattva "you who cannot control yourself, but are controlled by your passions and do naught but evil actions? Do you not know that when a boon is granted, it must be also fulfilled? I cannot accept a boon from you."

The son of Sudāsa bent his head in shame, and looking pleadingly at him said:

"Do not think too badly of me. Whatever may be the boons you choose to ask, I will grant them, even though it should cost me my life."

"Well then," said the Bodhisattva solemnly, "hear the boons which I crave!

1st. Take thou the vow of Truth,

2nd. Cease from injuring living beings,

3rd. Free all your prisoners,

4th. Never again partake of human flesh."

"I grant you the three first boons, O Prince of the silver tongue; but choose again the fourth boon, as I am not able to promise not to eat human flesh."

"Just so!" "said Sutasoma," did I not tell you that you could not grant boons? How can you give up injuring living beings if you can not give up the eating of human flesh? Shame on you? First to promise, even at the cost of your life, and now even the three granted boons have no value, with the fourth ungranted!" which is an outcome of the three."

The man-eater said sadly:

"How can I give up this habit, for the sake of which I gave up my kingdom and all that bound me to human society?"

The Bodhisattva answered:

"For this very reason you should give up this habit, which has caused you to lose your righteousness, your royal power, your pleasures, in one word—all. Besides, only the worst of men repent of having given. You granted me the boons willingly and now you refuse to keep your promise. Stop eating human flesh, and take meat examined by your physician and prepared by your cook. Satisfy your craving with such meat Do not be dominated by your passion, but be master of your desires. You who have conquered in war so many kings, can you not conquer your own passion? Are you such a coward that you cannot wage war against this one great evil desire? Think also of the next world, of your renown, and of the one who brought you up in love and honour even as his own son."

So convincing were the words of the Bodhisattva, so grand and beautiful the shining form before the man-eater, that he was moved to tears, and falling down before the prince and clasping his feet he exclaimed:—

"Truly you are my Deity, my Teacher. I will follow your commands, and never again eat of human flesh. You are the only living being who ever had compassion upon me, in spite of my evil-doings; you have conquered me by righteousness and by Truth. Humbly I bow my head, and kneel before you, my Teacher."

Then rising from his knees he said: "Come, let us free those hundred princes, captured by me, who await their death as sacrifice to the Demons."

Thus the princes were freed and radiant with joy they were conducted by Sutasoma to his own realm, where they were all established again in their own Kingdoms.

But the son of Sudāsa was a changed man. He remained with Sutasoma for a while, and then returned to his own kingdom, his family and friends, and reigned in righteousness and justice until the end.

Thus did the Bodhisattva teach by righteousness, by truth and virtue, bringing the most evil person from the path of evil to that of virtue.

XXV.

THE STORY OF SUPPĀRAKA.

The following story shows the power of Truth over winds and currents and even over any calamity.

The Bodhisattva, it is said, was once a clever pilot. But at that time of the world this meant a great deal, for there were no compasses by which to find out the ship's course; so a pilot, or a captain, had to know the fixed stars and the planets and the right time of sailing. Besides he had to study the colour of the sea and the nature of its bottom and the directions in which the fish swam. He had to know where sand-banks or rocks were situated, which might damage the ships; and he had to be always wakeful during the nights and be able to stand heat and cold and rain and sunshine. All these qualities were his, and Suppāraka, as the Bodhisattva was called, had all his life time conducted the merchant vessels to their various destinations.

The merchants, who secured his services for the conducting of their ships across the seas, considered themselves very fortunate and well they might for their ships were sure to return to their ports laden with riches. But now, Suppāraka was growing very old and feeble; also his eyesight was failing him, because it was affected by constant exposure to the brine of the sea. Suppāraka remained at home in his old age ; he did not guide ships any more, but he tried to instruct the young men who intended to become pilots themselves in the art of becoming real masters of the art of steering ships.

He was esteemed and honoured by everybody and often he was persuaded just to step on board the merchants' vessels for a little while, for the sake of bringing luck to them, even if he could not do service any longer.

One day, some merchants, who were trading with Gold-land, came to Supparaka's town and pleaded with him to come with them on their ship, in order to bring them a prosperous voyage.

He said to them : "What service can I do you? My body is feeble and my eye-sight is almost gone, on account of the hard labour I have done. Let me rest, and you go in peace on your voyage."

The merchants answered : "We know that you are old and that you cannot work, but we plead with you to come with us on our good ship ; for wherever you walk there prosperity comes. We want you to be with us in the dangers of the wide ocean which we have to cross. Be our protector and our guide, we entreat you!"

Out of compassion the Bodhisattva went on board their vessel, and with gratitude and happiness in their hearts the merchants started on their voyage.

All went well for seven days, when a high wind began to blow, and this wind continued

Suppāraka and the merchants.

all the time, till they came on their voyage to that part of the ocean, where Pâtâla, the abode of the Nāgas is. This is the great expanse of water called the 'Great Ocean,' to which it is hard to penetrate, and from which it is very difficult to return. Here the waters are never quiet; fish of enormous size haunt their depths, and the ship is the sport of the elements. But here are also the beds of precious stones on the bottom of the turbulent sea, and the foam of its storm-tossed waves forms flower-garlands of different hues.

Deep sapphire blue was the colour of the sea, just as if the sky had melted by the heat of the sun and were lying on the surface of the water, when the ships came to this Great Ocean, where nothing but sky and water was to be seen. No sail was in sight and they seemed to be alone, alone on the waste of water.

Almost four months had passed, and the high wind, which had been blowing all the time, turned into a terrific gale. Huge waves were breaking over the ship, which began trembling as if in fear. The Ocean took the appearance of the earth with its quivering mountains at the time of an earthquake. Clouds of greyish-blue, with flame-tongued lightning, like many-headed snakes, darkened the sun, and tremendous thunder claps shook the air.

Thus it went on till darkness closed over them and now the terror of the night, added to the uproar of the elements, brought dread and fear to almost all the inmates of the ship. Some prayed to their guardian gods, some sank down in indifference and only a few tried to avert danger by attending to their different duties.

The Bodhisattva was calm, and tried to comfort them, and said: "Are we not on the Great Ocean? You must not wonder that we are tossed about! Only by constancy and courage can we overcome difficulties. Set to work, by energy and firmness of mind we can overcome these trials. Let each of you perform his own special duty."

So the people on the ship followed his advice, and although fearing their destruction, they busied themselves with their various duties of fastening the sails and pulling the ropes tight and whatever they could do, to make the ship more secure.

But when they looked into the sea, they imagined they saw beings in silver armour, with big ugly noses, rolling about the waves, and fighting with each other.

The frightened men ran to Suppāraka, and exclaimed:

"Up they come and down they dive,
The men with sharp-edged noses.
On this sea, Suppāraka,
What name dost thou bestow?"

Suppāraka answered:

"This sea is Kuramalin called
Which means the 'hoof-garlanded.'
It kicks and wrecks the vessel mean
Whose name with theft is branded."

Suppāraka and the merchants on their ship.

Then he explained to the merchants that those beings were immense fish, not Demons, which were sporting in the rough waters. But he added, " We are far off from any shore and you must try to turn the ship."

The sailors tried to turn the ship, but the storm and the waves were too strong; the ship was driven forward in the same direction, evidently to its doom.

Before long they saw before them another sea and it was beautiful to look at, appearing to be covered with a sheet of fine white linen, sprinkled with silvery white foam. It looked as if moonbeams made fluid were floating on it.

The merchants wondered and said that this sea appeared to look at them with a laughing face.

" This ocean looks like milk or curd,
Like curdled milk or whey.
What is it called Suppāraka ?
Our question answer, pray ! "

Suppāraka answered:

" This Sea is Dadhimālin called
Or rather, Sea of curds
Its name is also Milky Sea,
And danger round it lurks.
Turn, turn the ship with all your might
For further going is not right."

The merchants made a great effort to change the course of the ship, but helplessly she was driven on: wind and current were too strong for human effort to have any effect on them.

So the unfortunate ship drifted on, evidently to ruin. And now they came to a sea which had amber-golden waves, like flames tinted with the colour of the rising sun.

The merchants ran to their Leader and cried out excitedly,

> " This ocean shineth like a fire
> Or like the Midday-Sun,
> What is it called Suppāraka?
> Answer our question, sire."

Supparaka answered :

> " This Sea is Agnimālin called
> Or Fire adorned Sea.
> The name is very much esteemed,
> For Gold its treasures be."

Again they were told to turn the ship; but it was impossible. On, on it rushed till the Merchants saw the waves change again into the colour of ripe Kusa-grass, studded with shining yellow topazes and blue sapphires, as if with flowers.

The Merchants ran again to their Leader and cried :

> " This ocean looks like Kusa-Grass
> Or a field of waving corn,
> What is it called Suppāraka?
> Answer your friends outworn,"

Suppāraka said :

> " Now we have Kusamālin found
> 'Tis called the Grass-green Sea
> Soon it will be too late to leave,
> For this Sea takes, but will not give."

But even with the greatest effort, the

Merchants could not turn the ship and they believed themselves lost.

Now the waves again changed and they turned green as if studded with emeralds, beryls and red corals. This sea looked like a meadow where different coloured waterlilies grow.

The Merchants, who had never seen anything like it, cried in fear :—

"This Sea looks like a Meadow green
With flowers of corals fair,
What may it be? Oh, Leader dear,
Tell us, we pray in fear,"

The Great Being, foreseeing the calamity which would have to befall the Merchants who had penetrated too far on their voyage. answered :—

" Soon Death will hold us in his grip
For your course you did not mend.
You are on Nalamālin's Sea,
The Red Sea near World's end."

The poor Merchants were overcome with fear as they were helpless. They were as if struck down by an unknown power. And yet the ship rushed on.

Then, just about the time when the sun kisses the Ocean and falls into it, they heard a dreadful noise, as if an immense bamboo-grove were on fire, or as if a sea in rage were falling down into an abyss, or as if hundreds of thunderclaps were united in one roar.

This was the culmination of everything

they had lived through, and all were paralysed with dread. They cried in utmost distress:

"With horrible, inhuman screams
The waves are whirling round.
Like a sunken pit this Ocean seems.
Pilot, its name expound.
Is Ganga, Queen of rivers angry with the worlds,
That she pours out her waters into depths unknown.
Is this the end, the end of all the World?

The Pilot groaned and cried:—

"You are now in Valabhāmukha,
Near the Whirl-pool at the Southern Pole,
This is the mouth-like door of Death
Called also famous Mara's-Mouth;
Now there's no help for all of you.
Death's hour has come for all the crew."

The merchants were silent with fear after this answer of their Leader.

Then they prayed and lamented and prepared themselves for death.

But some of them, having complete confidence in Suppāraka, came to him, and throwing themselves at his feet, they pleaded: "You, who have always had compassion for others, you, who always relieved from fear those who appealed to you, help us in our great distress. You, Wise One, rescue us, who are on the point of being swallowed up by Mara's-Mouth, like a portion of food. The Great Ocean will obey your orders, we know."

The Bodhisattva was moved by compassion and he answered: "There is one remedy left. Keep your minds fixed on me in prayer."

Then throwing his upper garment on one shoulder and bending his right knee, he made the great "Declaration of Truth" thus:

"Never since childhood's earliest days
Since, of myself aware,
I first attained intelligence,
I earnestly declare
I never purposely deprived
A being of its life.
By virtue of this Oath of mine
May our good ship in port arrive,
Safe home us merchants bear."

And so powerful was the appeal of the Bodhisattva, so true was the declaration he made, that wind and current obeyed his invocation and, although almost gripped in the fangs of Death, the ship suddenly turned and the reverse current and wind carried it now in the opposite direction.

Gladness filled the hearts of the occupants of the ship and deep was the veneration paid by them to the Leader, who had rescued them from the jaws of death.

Four months they had taken to get to the end of their voyage and now the good ship skimmed the sea like a bird with outspread wings, in joyous flight. The ship almost flew over the waves on its return voyage.

When the sun had sunk into the now calm ocean and the stars were sparkling in their heavenly splendour, Suppāraka called the sea-traders round him and told them that, while crossing the different seas, they should draw up sand and stones from the depth of the Ocean, at the places which he would indicate to them. "Thus you will ballast the ship and make her heavier to withstand an attack of storm or waves and, besides, this will bring you other advantages" he said.

Suppāraka's orders were obeyed. The ship was loaded with sand and stones from the different seas and during that one night she bounded so rapidly over the ocean, that by the next day they reached Bharukaccha, their destination and their home.

And behold! when the sun rose, the deck of the good ship was sparkling and glittering with thousands of emeralds, sapphires, beryls, coral, gold and silver. The supposed stones and the sand from the Khuramālin, Dadhimālin, Agnimālin and Kusamālin, were jewels and gold and silver.

The Bodhisattva, accepting the homage of the happy sea-traders, told them to be satisfied with the treasures they had gained on this one voyage, and advised them not to go on the sea again. They promised him faithfully that they would follow his advice and this promise was never broken. This was the Bodhisattva's last voyage in this incarnation as Suppāraka, the Pilot.

Through Truth the greatest calamity was averted in this case and through Truthfulness even now the greatest gain in life can be acquired.

N. B. [This story is very symbolical and the thoughtful reader will find many occult truths in it between the lines.]

XXVI.

THE STORY OF MAITRIBALA

In another of his incarnations, the Bodhisattva, then far on the road to Buddahood, was a king who was noble-minded and compassionate to such a degree that he was willing tc give his flesh and blood to five hungry Yakshas in order to save them from starvation and also to deliver his country from the ravages of these creatures.

King Maitribala had received this name on account of his strength and his kindness; for this name means "he whose strength is kindness." His sword was only an ornament, not needed for war, as all the kings of the surrounding countries were at peace with him.

In this land of order and happiness, where the law of righteousness reigned and where truthfulness, liberality and charity were practised by the people, who followed the example of their great king Maitribala, one day there appeared five Yakshas. They had been exiled from their fatherland by Kutera, their king, on account of some crime they had committed. So you see they must have been very wicked as they were exiled from that bad country which was full of crime.

These Yakshas were Ojokâras; that means they had the power of killing others by creating illness like consumption and fever, and they were just like a plague, which tries to take hold of and destroy the people.

These five Yakshas looked around in the country of king Maitribala and found contentment happiness, justice and cleanliness everywhere and, much as they tried, they could not succeed in creating any disease or any calamity.

They wondered, because they saw that the people did not possess learning to such a degree as to withstand their magic power of evil and they thought they must find out the reason of the power that protected the people and the land.

So the five Yakshas assumed the shapes of human beings, and they appeared as Brahmanas to a cowherd who was sitting under a shady tree near a jungle. This cowherd looked the picture of contentment. A wreath of wild forest-flowers crowned his head, he had put his long staff at his side and he was twisting a rope while singing in an under tone a song to himself.

As he was quite alone, they approached him and said, "How is it that you, a cowherd, sit here quite alone near the jungle where hardly any man comes. Are you not afraid to stay here quite by yourself?"

"Why should I be afraid?" laughed the cowherd.

"Well," said the Yakshas, "have you never heard about Rakshasas, or Yakshas, spirits who feed on the flesh of men?"

The cowherd laughed again and replied, "The people of this country are protected by a mighty Talisman so that even the Lord of the

The Cowherd and the five Yakshas.

Devas himself could not hurt them, even if he wanted to. How should we then fear the raw-flesh-eating goblins ? I wander as safely in these lonely jungles, as if I were in my own home."

Now the Yakshas became very curious and asked gently : "Will you tell us what this wonderful Talisman is which makes you so fearless and so content ?"

"You must have come from a very far country," said the cow-herd, laughing again, "if you do not know of the wonderful protection of this Talisman of ours. It is our King who is our Talisman. It is he whose face shines like the gentle moon, whose arms are like golden staves, whose eyes have the look of a powerful bull, and whose broad chest seems cut out of Mount Meru. And," the cowherd continued, "it is only a wonder to me that you have not heard of the fame of our king. The people of your country cannot have been searching for virtue or perhaps their good Karma has left them, that the renown of our king has never reached them. But for you there is some good fortune left, for now you have heard about our king, you can go and see him yourselves."

"Tell us, before we leave you," said the five Yakshas, "can your king really protect his whole country against evil spirits ?"

"Our great king has this power by his noble-mindedness, his friendliness, his righteousness and his compassion. Many other virtues are his and therefore no calamities can come to his country and his people. I am only an ignorant cowherd and cannot give you much information. Go yourselves to our capital and see how the people live there, how they keep precepts of good conduct, how they honour worthy guests and how they praise the virtues of our great king."

The Yakshas were moved rather by anger against the good king than by love for him, for they saw that his great virtues were more powerful, than their magic. But they did not show this to the happy cowherd. They told him that they were on their way to see the great king, who was the Talisman of his whole country.

So the five Yakshas, in the garb of Brahmanas, came to the audience hall of king Maitribala; with the intention of doing him harm. they asked for some food. The good king gave orders at once to feed the five Brahmanas with the best food that could be prepared for such guests.

Delicious dishes, good enough for a king's table, were put before them ; but the so called Brahmanas turned away their faces and said that they were accustomed to other food, and that they would not eat what was put before them.

Then the king, when he was told about this, went himself and asked the disguised Yakshas what food they liked, so that it could be given to them.

The answer which the king received was a

strange and disgusting one, for the guests said. "Raw human flesh just cut from the body and fresh human blood: that is our food, Oh Lotus-eyed king! And so we ask you, who always give what is asked for, to give us that food and drink and nothing else. We are Yakshas and took the shapes of Brahmanas only in order to get near you."

After saying this they resumed their Yaksha shapes and stood before the king with their hideous bodies and their large teeth and grinning mouths, to the astonishment and horror of the king and his attendants.

What could the king do under these circumstances? He could see at once that they were not human beings but goblins of some kind, and their large teeth and round big mouths showed that they were raw meat-eaters and that they would not be contented with the drinking of water like the other beggars who were fed by him. What could he do? How could he get them the food and drink they wanted?

The king, in his compassion even for the hungry Yakshas, could not find any other way out of this trouble than to feed them with his own flesh; for how could he injure anybody else? That seemed to him the least wrong; for how could he send anybody away who had asked him for food, without satisfying his hunger?

So the king said to the Yakshas: "Would the blood and the flesh from this body of mine, which I wear for the benefit of my people, be of any use to you?"

The Yakshas understood very well what the king meant but they could hardly believe their ears and they said: "After the wretched hungry beggars have confided their troubles—from that time it is the giver who ought to know what to do."

This answer showed their evident willingness to accept the offer and the king at once ordered his physicians to come and open five of his veins so that the thirsty Yakshas could drink his blood.

But the physicians and the attendants of good king Maitribala were horrified beyond expression and they besought and pleaded with the king to take their own flesh and blood and not his to feed these wretched Yakshas.

The ministers said: "They have no power to injure your people, as long as you are their father and protect them."

The king answered: "If I were faint-hearted how could I protect my people? Besides, they have asked me for food, and as I have it. I must give it. My body is there for the benefit of the poor. I cannot bear to see the sufferings of my enemies; how do you think I could bear to see you suffer my friends? No, no, do not hinder me from granting this uncommon demand. Self love would be practised did I not keep my promise to give the food requested by these five Yakshas."

So the king had five veins of his body opened by his physicians and he invited the five Yakshas to make him glad by accepting the desired drink. The Yakshas drank the blood of the good king while his face shone with gladness, and because of his bodily strength and divine protection his body did not get faint nor his mind troubled.

When the Yakshas had satisfied their thirst the king took his sharp sward, which had never been used, and cut five pieces of flesh out of his body, which he presented to the Yakshas. And again his gladness in performing this sacrifice overcame the bodily pain so that even the cruel hearts of the Yakshas softened and they called out: " Enough, enough," when they saw how calmly and serenely the king was killing himself by degrees for their sakes.

So these monsters, filled with admiration for the saintly king, bowed down before him, with tears of remorse in their once cruel eyes and said: " Your glory, O King, will be proclaimed everywhere and even Hamsa, the Immortal Bird,* will wish to abide with you. Even heaven might be jealous at seeing such heroism on earth. We are utterly distressed at having asked for such a boon, but this has brought about our salvation. We will turn our steps and live better lives. May we be allowed to ask you one question before we turn our steps towards the new Path ? "

---

* The Immortal Bird—or Hamsa, sometimes called the Swan, is a symbol of Immortality. It is said that the highly developed person with whom this Bird remains will live for ever.

The king consented and the Yakshas asked: "Do you, O king, wish to possess the whole of the earth or the rank of Kubera or Indra or the absorption into Brahma that you do such penance?"

The king answered: "Neither the possession of the whole earth nor the rank of the Gods nor the destruction of suffering in myself is my aim for they are not eternal. My aim is to help the poor and the wicked, to save creatures from the distress of re-birth with its trouble of old age, sickness and death and to attain all Knowledge by these my meritorious actions."

The Yakshas were overcome by these words and exclaimed: "Surely such exertions will save all creatures! May you pardon us that which we have done in ignorance and may you help us and pray for us when you have attained the high state of Salvation."

The king, seeing that these former monsters were really converted and had lost their hardheartedness, answered: "Do not be distressed any more, you have even helped me on the way to Salvation, for there is no other road for those who follow the Path of Righteousness. I shall not forget you, for you are my companions on that same road, and when once I have attained "Perfect Wisdom" my first teaching shall be to you * If now you want

* It is said that the five Ascetics with whom the Bodhisattva lived in the forest and to whom afterwards he preached the first sermon after becoming the Buddha, were the Yakshas of this story, to whom he promised to preach, after attaining the Perfect Wisdom.

some advice from me, then I say unto you, "Avoid like poison the 'sins of doing harm to others, of coveting the wives and the goods of others, of talking evil and of drinking intoxicating liquors."

The now humble Yakshas bowed, walked round the king from right to left and dis appeared.

But King Maitribala was not forgotten by the Celestials during the distress of his wounds, for the Earth trembled and Mount Meru* shook and clouds of flowers showered down on the good king and even the great Ocean, like a powerful auxiliary prince stood up ready to defend his ally.

The king of the Devas rushed to the Royal residence to help the king in his suffering. Here he found everybody distressed except the king himself, who in spite of his pains was calm and content. Sakra was astounded seeing this and exclaimed: "Verily Earth has obtained a Protector in Thee, O King, who practiceth virtue to perfection. Thou surely hast reached the height of piety." He applied divine and medical herbs to the wounds of king Maitribala which healed them as if by magic. In a short time the body of the king was as strong as it had been before. Then Sakra went back to his heavenly abode blessed by the adoring subjects of the pious king Maitribala.

---

* Mount Meru is said to be the mountain on which the worlds rest.

This story teaches that those who are really compassionate do not mind giving away all that they possess, even if it be their own bodies. They cannot see others suffer but do not mind suffering themselves if by doing so they can help others.

It also teaches that by the practice of giving, even long before the Bodhisattva became the Lord Buddha, he converted vicious beings like the five Yakshas into good ones.

XXVII.

THE STORY OF THE KING OF THE CIBIS

Once, in his earthly wanderings, seeking perfection, the Bodhisattva was born as the son of the king of the Cibis. He had such a quick understanding that he grew up to be a master of all sciences and arts as well as of all virtues. When he became king he ruled his subjects as a father his children.

As he was very wealthy and noble-hearted, he tried to supply all the needs of the poor of his country, and they and the mendicants filled his palace every day.

He was so full of love and charity for his subjects that his country abounded with alms-houses which were filled with necessities for the comfort and support of their inmates. In this way he poured forth the rain of his gifts as did the clouds in the Treta-Yuga which of old supplied the people with food.*

Each suppliant received according to his needs, and the king looked with beaming eyes on those who left the palace with happy faces. It seemed as if he as the giver was even more happy than they as the receivers, and they came in streams to him and all returned from the palace loaded with gifts. But the king was not satisfied with giving his wealth away. He wished that somebody would ask him for a part of his body, so that he could show that he would be willing to give that away too.

When Mother Earth became aware of this lofty thought of the king, she trembled with joy, and Maha-meru, the Lord of the mountains, began to shake.

Then Sakra, the king of the Devas, enquired about the cause of this unusual shaking of the earth, and when he heard of the divine thought of the king of the Cibis, who was willing to give even a part of his body to any needy person, he was amazed and thought: "Can it really be possible that this king is so noble-minded and charitable as to be willing to give his own limbs away? I must try him."

---

* See "The Laws of Manu in the Light of Theosophy" by Bhagavan Das. "Then rain fell from the skies, rain of liquids not exactly the same as the waters of to-day, but milky and full of food."

So when the king was sitting again on his throne in his audience-hall, after the usual summons had been given for all the poor and needy to come and receive the desired gifts, streams of beggars and needy people appeared and received silver, gold, jewels, cloth, paddy and grains, everyone according to his needs.

Among the crowd of beggars appeared Sakra, the king of the Devas, in the form of an old blind Brahman. Leaning on his staff, with bent head he stood before the King, who looked at him with compassion and friendliness.

The royal attendants enquired as to his wants; but he drew quite close to the king, and, after blessing him, said: "I have come here from afar, O King, a blind old man, for I have heard of your great compassion. I beg of you one of your eyes, as the other will suffice you wherewith to rule your kingdom."

The king was delighted at this request, having long wished for the opportunity of being the one who might sacrifice his body. But as the request was so very unusual, he doubted whether he had understood aright, so he asked the blind Brahman, "Who has told you to ask me for my eye? No one surely would be very willing to part with one of his eyes"

The Brahman answered: "Sakra, the King of the Devas, has instructed me to ask you for your eye. He told me that you would

The blind Brahman asks the King for one of his eyes.

give it to me, and I hope I shall not be disappointed."

When the king heard this, he thought that through the power of Sakra the blind man might regain his eyesight, and he said, "Brahman, I will fulfill your wish. You have asked for one of my eyes, I will give you both."

The King's councillors, understanding that the king really intended to give away his eyes, begged the him with tears not to carry his charity so far as to willingly become blind. "Besides," they argued, "how can the eyes of one person be put into the head of another? If divine power can bestow sight, why give away your eyes?"

"Besides, what is the use of eyesight to a poor man? He will then witness the abundance of others. and hence become sad. Give him instead some money, and let him go in peace!"

The king replied in a gentle voice, "He who has promised a gift and breaks his promise is the worst of men. You say also that if the divine power can give back the Brahman his eye-sight it is not necessary to give my eyes. Let me point out to you that different means must be used to carry a purpose into effect and I believe that my eyes are needed to accomplish this effect on the twice-born, therefore do not hinder me in this unusual form of charity."

The ministers further remonstrated, but the king said, "The very thing asked for must be given. An unwished for gift does no good. It is not that I try to win the realm of the whole earth nor heaven nor glory but it is with the intention of becoming a Saviour of the world that I now give my eyes that this man's request may be fulfilled."

Then the king ordered his physician to take one of his eyes carefully out of his head, unhurt, and give it to the blind Brahman. And to the wonder of the king and his people, the king's eye filled the empty eye-socket of the Brahman, and shone out in splendour.

When the king saw this with his one remaining eye, he was delighted, and ordered his physician to take out the other and give it to the Brahman. The pious king's face now looked like a lotus pond without the lotus, but the Brahman walked off with two sound eyes, making deep obeisance to the now blind king.

Everywhere in the palace and in the town tears of sorrow were shed; But Sakra, the King of the Devas, was filled with admiration and satisfaction, seeing the king unshaken in his intention of attaining Supreme Wisdom, and he resolved that this marvellously good king should not endure very long the great hardship of blindness.

When the wounds which had been caused by the operation upon the eyes had healed, and the king was one day sitting meditating near a lotus pond in his garden. where balmy breezes were blowing and where the

The King gives away his eyes.

flower-laden bushes showered their petals on the pond; king Sakra appeared before him and said "I am Sakra, the King of the Devas: choose one boon, holy Prince."

The blind king, who was always ready to give, but who did not know how to ask for a boon, was very much astonished at this and said: "I have great wealth, a large army, and the love of my subjects, but blindness makes me wish for death, for I cannot see the glad face of the poor after fulfilling their wishes."

"Do you still think of the beggars," Sakra said, "after they have brought you to this sad state of blindness?"

Then the king replied, "Having always worshipped Truth, I now make my appeal to her. If I be speaking Truth in saying that the supplications of the needy are as sweet and as irresistible to me now that I am sightless as they were before, when I could enjoy the sight of their happy faces, then hearken, O Eternal Truth, and justify me by giving me back one of my eyes."

As soon as he had uttered these words, by the power of his utter truthfulness, and by the merit of his unfailing charity, one of his eyes came back to him, and in his happiness at seeing again with one eye, he exclaimed:

"I speak again the truth in saying that I felt delight only at giving away both eyes when asked for one alone. Now, to prove my truthfulnes, I adjure Truth to weigh me in her balance, and give me back my second eye."

Hardly had the pious king finished speaking, when his second eye came back to him and he could see all the beauty around him and could look again on the delighted faces of the poor who gathered around him.

When this miracle happened the earth shook with gladness, the sun shone in clear splendour, flowers showered down on the saintly king, and all nature rejoiced. All creatures were glad that their protector had regained his eyesight, and soft voices sang "Hail to the king of Righteousness and Compassion."

Then Sakra spoke to the Bodhisattva, and said, "I knew of your intention of being ready even to give your limbs away, and I was the Brahman who tested you. I have given you back your eyes, and with your eyes I also give you divine sight; you have now the power to see in all directions for over one hundred yojanas.*

After saying this, Sakra disappeared. Then the king was brought in procession to his decorated capital, Arittha, and all his subjects rejoiced and followed him to the audience-hall in his palace, and here he preached the Law to them, taking for his text, the account of his own experience.

Thus he reigned wisely until the day of his death, giving all his wealth to the poor and sorrowful.

*** Yojana—equal to 16 miles.**

Wealth is a contemptible thing, yet it has one virtue, and that is that it can be given away by him who possesses it for the welfare of other creatures. Then only does it become a treasure.

XXVIII.

THE STORY OF MAHABODHI

The following story shows that the compassion of the Bodhisattva is so great, that it does not diminish even if those who have been benefactors to him at first turn against him later on.

Once the Bodhisattva was a wandering ascetic, after a most virtuous life as a householder. During his life as a householder he had acquired all that learning which was valued in the world, and when he retired from the life of the world and became an ascetic he studied the law-books and became a Master of the Law.

Thus learned in every science he was honoured and sought after by everybody and his reputation became very great.

In his wanderings he came near the borders of the land of a king who had heard a great deal about him and who wished very much to have him live in his country for a while. So he built a house in his own pleasure garden for him and, when the Bodhisattva came to his capital, the king met him very reverently and asked him to come to live in the house prepared for him.

The king himself waited on him and listened with great attention to his teachings, which were to prepare him for walking on the Road of Salvation. Every day the king listened to the lessons of wisdom taught by the Bodhisattva and he became wiser and better every day. But the ministers and counsellors of the king became jealous of the Bodhisattva, although he treated them with all due respect according to their learning and their position. They were afraid that they would lose their influence on the king, who drank in with eagerness the wisdom that came from the Bodhisattva's lips.

As the ministers were unable to argue with the Bodhisattva in open contest, they tried to undermine his authority with the king by making him suspicious. They said that the king ought not to put too much confidence in this wandering Monk Bodhi, who, they firmly believed, was a spy from some rival king, who used the smooth tongue of this clever fellow to induce the king to leave the life of royal and military duties which are necessary for a king and take upon himself the vows of a religious life. "Thus," they said to the king "the material interests of your people would be neglected and it would be easy for a rival, king to conquer your kingdom."

Such words, often repeated, under the plea of love and attachment to the king, by his ministers and counsellors, could not fail to making some impression on the king, who began to distrust the Bodhisattva. He began to neglect him in his personal wants and he did not pay so much attention as before to his teachings.

The Bodhisattva, in his compassion, did not mind that his cooked rice became coarser every day and his gruel thinner, but, when the king became cooler and less attentive to his teachings, he felt that he had lost the king's confidence. So he took his triple bamboo-staff, his water pot, strainer and other belongings of his ascetic life and made himself ready to leave the king's house. When the king heard of this, he came to the Bodhisattva and asked him the reason of his leaving so suddenly. The Bodhisattva answered: "It is not suddenly that I leave, I have a good reason for so doing. It is not the small matter of being neglected that has vexed me, but I see that your Majesty has ceased to be a vessel of righteousness and that suspicion has crept into your heart against me."

While he was thus speaking, the king's favourite dog came up to the Bodhisattva and instead of lying down in friendly way at his feet as usual, he snarled at him and opened his mouth wide as if he wanted to bite him.

"This dog," said the Bodhisattva, "can testify to my words. Formerly he was friendly towards me, and now he shows suspicion. He must have heard some harsh words spoken of me. This is generally the way of servants who eat the bread of their masters, and who thus try to please them."

The king became ashamed, for he saw the truth of the Bodhisattva's words, and bowing down low to him he said: "It is true, my ministers have used harsh words against you, but I ask your forgiveness and plead with you not to leave me."

The Bodhisattva answered. "With a heart full of resentment and anger, I do not leave, for I remember all the benefits I have received at your hands: but seeing that all the honours heaped up on me formerly have lost their loveliness, the time might come when I would be turned out altogether. So I think it is better to go willingly now, since my teachings have lost their effect on Your Majesty!"

The King replied: "If Your Reverence has decided to go, may I plead that some day you will come back?"

"Your Majesty," answered the Bodhisattva, "I cannot positively promise to return to you, as I am a wanderer in the world. I can only express my wish that I may see you again some day."

After these words the Bodhisattva took up his staff and wandered off. He passed through villages and towns, and many a time he was asked to remain. But as he felt that he wanted to live alone, he settled down in a forest, where he devoted himself to meditation. Very soon he attained Dhyâna* and Abhiññâ † (the Iddhis), and one day, when, in his compassion for the king, whom he left under the bad influence of his councellors and ministers, he directed his divine vision to him, he saw that the poor king was misled altogether by those who surrounded him and that his mind was becoming bewildered by the conflicting advice of his counsellors.

One of them wanted to make the king believe that there was no cause for the existence of the world and what is in the world. Another wanted to make him see in the God Ishvara the cause of everything. A third explained to him that the world was the result of former actions and that personal energy could not modify it. Another again wanted him to live only for the pleasures of the world, saying that death was annihilation. Yet another taught him that a king was a being vested with absolute power and that he should look upon men as trees, to be sacrificed at the will of their king.

So the king was distracted with conflicting opinions and the Bodhisattva foresaw that in a short time he would lose his goodness of heart and follow the wrong doctrines taught to him.

In his compassion he meditated to find out the best way to free the king from these

---

* Dhyâna-Superhuman consciousness.

† Abhiññâ, Iddhis or higher powers, obtained by the exercise of the Dhyâna.

false ideas and he found out how he could help him.

He went to work and created in his own hermitage, by the force of his supernatural power, the shape of a huge ape, whose skin he stripped off and whose body he made disappear again. He put this monkey-skin on his body and thus he appeared at the entrance gate of the king's palace.

The king was just then sitting in his audience hall surrounded by all his ministers and counsellors, dealing out justice and hearing the petitions of his subjects. The Bodhisattva entered the hall, without being hindered by the watchers, and, when the king saw him, he came down from his throne, greeted him reverently and offered him a high seat, which he accepted.

Now the king was very curious about the monkey-skin worn by the Bodhisattva and he asked him how he had got this fine skin.

The Bodhisattva answered: "I did not receive it from anybody, I got it myself; I had only thin straw on which to sleep, and to do my religious exercises, and my body suffered from it, and when I saw a big monkey in my hermitage I killed him and took his skin."

When the king heard this he did not say anything, but he was astonished to hear this answer. But his ministers and counsellors, who had a grudge against the Bodhisattva, thought it a good opportunity to make the

Mahabodhi Preaches to the King.

king distrust him, and pointing to the Bodhisattva they said to the king: "Does his Majesty see now how much this monk loves his religion? It is wonderful that an ascetic, emaciated by his penance, has the strength to kill the huge monkey whose skin he wears now; may his penance be successful."

When the Bodhisattva heard these sarcastic words, he turned to the minister who wanted to make the king believe that there was no cause for the existence of the world and what is in the world, and said to him; "If that which you teach is true, that there is no cause for the existence of the world and that the universe is the product of inherent properties, why do you blame me that I killed the monkey, as he died in consequence of his mortal nature? But if I did wrong in killing him, then you acknowledge that an external cause brought on his death and you must give up your teaching of non-causality. If you insist in your doctrine of no-cause, well then there is no reason for the death of the monkey. And why then should you blame me?"

The minister did not answer, because he could not say anything against this argument.

Then turning to the teacher of the doctrine that Ishvara is the cause of everything he said: "And you, my friend, should not blame me either, for you say that the Lord is the cause of everything. Then the Lord is also the cause of the death of the monkey and why should you blame me for it? If the Lord is the performer of everything (as you say) then he is also the performer of all sins. Then if the belief in the Supreme Being is accompanied by faith and by devotion, and if He is the cause of everything, then He had intended the death of the monkey and you must not blame me for his murder."

The minister was struck dumb by these arguments and did not say a single word in answer.

Turning to the third counsellor, who was an adherent of the doctrine that the world was the result of former actions and that personal energy could not modify it, the Bodhisattva continued:

"Neither ought you to blame me for the murder of the monkey, for, according to your teachings, everything is the consequence of former actions, and so the death of the monkey was the consequence of his former bad actions and I was only the instrument used for producing the punishment which he deserved. Further, if you say old actions are always the cause of fresh actions, then nobody could ever reach emancipation. Thus good and evil fortune would depend exclusively on former deeds. For what reason do you think then that I caused the death of the monkey?"

The counsellor could not answer this question and the Bodhisattva smilingly spoke to the friend of the king who believed only in annihilation and said: "I wonder that you find a reason to blame me, for if you really believe in no existence after death, in the annihilation of everything, then what does it matter whether one kills a man or a monkey? There is no punishment after death, as there is no existence after death, and so it does not matter whether one lives a good or a bad life. Why should one care for the opinion of others and why should one lead a virtuous life if with death all is finished? So if you really believe in annihilation, why should you censure me because I killed a monkey?"

Silence again from the adherent of the doctrine of annihilation!

Then the Bodhisattva turned to the minister who taught the doctrine of the absolute power of kings and he said: "How can you blame me for the killing of that monkey, whose skin I wanted for my own benefit. Do you not teach that deeds either good or evil can be performed for the sake of material interest? If it is allowed for the sake of personal interest that even father or mother, wife or child, brother and sister may be killed and kings may use men like trees, why should I not kill a monkey whose skin is useful to me? I only followed the policy which you teach in your doctrine."

All were abashed and the Bodhisattva saw that the king was won over to his teachings and that the present ministers and the whole assembly were full of admiration for the Guru, whose arguments could not be answered even by the learned ones present.

Then he turned to the king and said gently: "Your Majesty has heard my arguments and has seen that, even if I had killed the monkey, I should be justified for this deed according to the teachings of your ministers. But the fact is I never killed a monkey or any living being. By my power of creation I formed the shape of a monkey, whose skin I wanted for this conversation and teaching here."

Speaking thus he dematerialized before their eyes the monkey-skin which he wore and seeing that all were convinced of his words he said: "Do you think that I could have killed any living being, I who believe that all things produced are the result of cause? I act by my own free will and I believe in another world after this one. I know that a man is responsible for his own actions, I am compassionate to all living beings.

"A man's creed, whether it be a true or a false one, is the motive of his doings, and you find out the character of the man when you see his actions. Therefore false doctrines must be abandoned and right ones followed.

"Always seek the company of virtuous people, not of the wicked. I know there are some monks who go about like wolves in sheeps' clothing, and those are the ones who ruin simple people. They preach false doctrines which kill the people's hearts, as the bite of a poisonous snake kills the body.

Therefore a king must avoid the company of those who are not noble like unto himself, for even the full-moon loses her loveliness, when covered by dark rain-clouds. Practise virtue, O King ! and through your example virtue will be the watch-word of your people. Follow the Path of Righteousness, follow the Dharma and the Vinaya and your people will also keep on the path which leads to salvation. Purify your conduct and be charitable to everyone, O King ! and may you thus rule for a long time to the happiness of yourself and your people."

Thus the Bodhisattva taught Righteousness and Truth to the King and his attendants and then he lifted himself up into the air, and returned to his forest hermitage.

The king and his attendants never forgot the teachings of the Bodhisáttva, and Peace, Happiness and Righteousness ruled in this King's country who reigned in justice and compassion for a long time over his contented subjects.

XXIX.

THE STORY OF KSHANTIVĀDIN

In this incarnation, tne Bodhisateva was an ascetic and very highly developed. He had great repute as a preacher and he not only preached but also practised endurance and forbearance. His real name was soon forgotten among the people, who called him Kshantivādin (the preacher of forbearance) and by this name he was known every where.

He lived in a very lonely part of a forest. But this place was lovely and looked like a garden. It was near a pond of clear water in which white and blue lotuses grew, surrounded by flowering shrubs and fruit-trees. This forest was considered a holy place and virtuous people made pilgrimages to it and Kshantivādin always received them very kindly and preached to them sermons on forbearance.

One very hot summer day the king of the country thought that he would find cooling shade in the forest, and he went there with his wives and attendants in great number. The beautiful ladies were decorated with jewels and flowers and were anointed with such sweet smelling perfumes, that even the bees were attracted to them. The king was enjoying the fun of seeing his wives gathering flowers and dancing and singing and playing in the water and their chattering and the jingle of their bracelet-anklets was even louder than the crying of the cuckoo and the screaming of the peacocks. Such a merry-making in the forest was seldom seen there and even the birds in the trees wondered and were silent. At last the king got tired of all this fun and had his luxurious couch brought by his attendants

The sleeping King.

and placed in a natural arbour in the forest and there he lay down to sleep.

When his wives saw that he was asleep they left him quietly and roamed about in the forest, as they were quite enchanted with its beauty. They were followed by their female slaves, who were bearing the royal umbrella, the fan and the royal seat after them as signs of their royal birth. Although they wore plenty of flower wreaths and flowers in their hair and ears, they stripped all the bushes and plucked all the flowers which came in their way, and the road they had walked over was strewn with poor half-withered flower petals.

Thus the group of flower-bedecked ladies came near the hermitage of Kshantivādin who was sitting under a tree cross-legged, meditating on some profound problem. He looked so gentle, beautiful and kind, that the whimsical women became awestruck. They ceased their chattering and dancing and sitting down in a half-circle round him asked him to give them the benefit of his teachings. Kshantivādin welcomed them graciously and began preaching a sermon to them which was according to their understanding and which might produce some good in them. He told them that if anybody had attained the state of a human being having a strong healthy body, he must not neglect doing good actions every day for he would never be quite happy if he were not purified by charity.

"The one," the Bodhisattva said, "who is virtuous and charitable will be visited by bliss like the sea in rainy season by the rivers. Blossoms are the ornaments of bushes and trees, but the real jewels of human beings are virtues. Karma produces the stations in life, and health or illness, therefore everybody must avoid wickedness, for by doing so they find the road to happiness. Fire is extinguished by coming in contact with a great river, and so forbearance kills the fire of lust in the heart of a human being. Forbearance is the highest aim of a king and the richest blossom of the fruit of asceticism."

Thus the Bodhisattva preached to the queens who listened eagerly and all had forgotten their play. They resolved to practise that forbearance of which the ascetic spoke in such eloquent terms.

Meanwhile the king had awakened from his sleep and looking around could not see any of his wives near him. He got up from his couch rather crossly, for he was accustomed to have some of the queens always at his side. He asked his female attendants where his wives had gone, and he heard that they were roaming about in the forest, accompanied by their slaves. So he followed their track, which was easily found, as it was strewn with flowers and branches which they had pulled off in their play. On he walked with his female warriors and slaves till he came to the hermitage of the ascetic and saw to his dismay his wives seated in a semicircle

The King in search of the Queens

round Kshantivādin, who was sitting under a tree preaching a sermon tc them.

At this sight the king became very angry and jealous, and having already a grudge against this saintly man, he became so furious that he rushed towards the ascetic. Beads of perspiration were rolling down his face and with eyes full of wrath he exclaimed : "Hypocrite, how darest thou look upon my wives."

His attendants tried to call the king's attention to the fact that he was speaking to the great Muni Kshantivādin, who had purified his mind long since by penance.

But the king would not listen but called out : "I will punish this hypocrite for his false godliness and will show the people what he really is." With these words he snatched his sword which was carried behind him by his female sword-bearer, and unsheathed it, ready to strike the Bodhisattva.

His wives, frightened by the loud words and angry looks surrounded him and pleaded with him, not to injure the holy man ;

But the king was so angry that he did not pay any attention to their prayers. He motioned them away furiously saying : "This man has cast his looks on my wives, he only preaches forbearance but he does not practise it. He shall be punished."

With these words he stood before the Muni, who kept his face calm and was not frightened, although the king stood facing him with his sword drawn, ready to strike. The king only got more angry and said : "How well he can play the hypocrite, even now wanting me to believe that he is a holy man."

The Bodhisattva was not angry when he heard these words but he said gently: "I am sorry that Your Majesty does not allow me to give the welcome which I always grant to everybody who comes to me. Your Majesty should first try to get an insight into my failure of forbearance, if I have any, before threatening me. I am in your forest, in the penance grove and ought to be protected by your arm against anybody who comes to molest me, and now you take up arms yourself against me. Is it my fault that your wives came here and requested me to teach them? My teaching has done them no harm and I am sure you have no cause to be full of anger towards me, which is not becoming to a king."

But the king could not be conquered by these mild words and he said: "If you are not a hypocrite, but really an ascetic who does not care for life, why do you plead with me to practise forbearance?"

The Bodhisattva answered; "For your own sake I ask you to practise forbearance, for if you kill me, you will lose your good reputation and you will lose the merit of Righteousness.

Scornfully turning to the Bodhisattva the king exclaimed: "Let me see your forbearance," and with one stroke from his sharp sword he struck off the hand of the ascetic which was stretched out towards him.

Still the Bodhisattva did not curse the king, but he was very sad as he saw the misfortune which would befall the king after this horrible deed. And, like a physician who has given up his patient as hopeless, he was silent.

The king only got more exasperated than before, seeing the forebearance of the saintly ascetic, and he shouted : "And so I will cut off your other hand and your limbs also till death comes to you, if you do not cease from your deceit."

The Bodhisattva knew that nothing could help the king and he was silent. And the king cut off his arms, his ears, his nose, and his feet. But the Bodhisattva did not complain. He knew his body must die and he was ready. Only the wickedness of the king troubled him.

Then the king turned his back on the dying Arhat, with a wild fever burning in his heart, and before he had left the garden of the hermitage the earth opened, flames came out of it and the king was swallowed up.

A violent earthquake and fearful rumbling followed and the royal attendants, fearing for their lives also, ran to the dying Bodhisattva, whose power they knew ; and bowing down before him they implored him not to curse them for the sake of the one wicked king. They knew that his curse might destroy the whole country if he so wished.

But the dying saint comforted them and

said: "Only pity have I for the wicked king, who brings upon himself his own punishment. We all have to die anyhow and I have lost my body many a time in different ways, and I am ready to lose it now without losing that forbearance which I have practised so often. I have no desire for revenge. Go home in peace."

Thus the Bodhisattva lost his body in this incarnation. In spite of all the cruelty of the king, no bodily pain could make him lose his forbearance.

If it had been possible he would have saved the king from the consequences of his wickedness.

XXX.

THE STORY OF VESSANTARA

There lived once in India in the land called Jayatura a king named Sandumaha. He was renowned on account of his righteousness, his valour and his kindness. He was also very learned and he possessed the love of his subjects, who were safe under his rule and could practise their trades in peace.

King Sandumaha honoured arts and sciences and encouraged their pursuit. His subjects were content and happy under his strong yet just rule.

Vessantara on a holiday.

The Bodhisattva was born as his son Vessantara, who grew up as a marvel of virtue and learning. All the qualities which make a perfect man seemed united in the heir apparent, and his father trusted him with a good many duties of government, which he fulfilled perfectly.

Vessantara practised charity, the greatest virtue, to perfection and the only war in which he indulged was the war against hunger and thirst, sickness and poverty, and against these calamities he shot off his arrows of charity. Every gift which he gave was accompanied with kind words, and poor Brahamanas and beggars blessed him a thousand times for all he did for them.

On Poya-Days he observed all the prescribed rules and after bathing and putting on white clothes, he used to mount his favourite white elephant, an embodiment of vigour and sagacity and ride around to all the almshouses in the great city, to see that the guests of charity were properly cared for. His face shone out in joy when he saw that the sick and the poor were well taken care of.

The fame of Vessantara's charitableness was spread everywhere by the mendicants; and when in a neighbouring country a king who was jealous of him, heard that the young prince never refused to give anything for which he was asked, he sent some of his men in the garb of Brahmanas to try and rob Vessantara of his splendid elephant.

So when the prince, on a Poya-Day, was inspecting his alms-halls again, riding on his great elephant, the Brahmanas sent by the jealous king placed themselves in the road before him with outstretched arms, mumbling blessings on him. The prince stopped his elephant and in a kind voice asked them what were their wants.

"Knowing of your great love of charity and seeing your excellent elephant," answered the Brahmanas, "we have become beggars, and as you are wont to give what the beggars ask of you, we ask you to give us your elephant."

The prince was astonished at this request because he could not see what the Brahmanas wanted with his splendid elephant. He thought: "This must be a trick of some covetous king, who wants to have what he has no right to possess. But still how can I refuse this request, which is an unusual one? I have always been ready to give what has been asked from me."

So, subduing the thought that the giving away of the Royal Elephant was not according to the teachings of Political Wisdom which is next to Righteousness, he got down from his elephant, which, decorated with gold cloth and carrying a golden seat, looked like an autumn-cloud with a bright ray of the sun striking on it. He lifted his golden pitcher high up and pouring the water of donation on the hands of the Brahmanas, he gave ver

Vessantara gives away his elephant.

his elephant to them and walked back on foot to his palace.

When the subjects of king Sandumaha heard of this, they became very angry; and the ministers and attendants and the eldest of the Brahmanas came to the king and said: "O King, how can you allow the fortune of your kingdom to be carried away? In giving away the Royal Elephant who is worth more than all elephants together, who is feared by all kings and who has brought victory to the country, your son has given away part of your kingdom. Gold, cloth and food are what the Brahmanas need; but to give away the best elephant is going too far. Forbearance in this case is not right. The prince should be punished."

King Sandumaha loved his son very much, but he could not help seeing that he had acted against the teachings of Political Wisdom, and he told his Ministers that he would order his son to stop this passion for unreasonable charity.

But King Sandumaha's subjects were not satisfied with this and they said: "Your son, O King, is not fit to become your successor, because he loves only generosity and charity and not governing the country with a strong arm. A prince who can win renown with his warlike arm, ought to sit on the throne of his father, and not one who undermines the strength of his country by too great a passion for charity. His subjects request the great King Sandumaba to send his son Prince Vessantara to the Penance-grove on Mount Vanka, where he may think over his lack of the knowledge of Political Wisdom."

The king was very much distressed hearing the harsh words of the spokesman of his people, who really only spoke because he foresaw calamities which must follow on the adoption of a false policy. And the king, heaving a deep sigh, answered: "If this is the wise decision of my people, be it so! but my son must have one day and one night for preparation before his exile."

The king called his oldest minister and sent him to his son to tell him what had happened. This old man loved Vessantara very much and, bathed in tears, he threw himself at the feet of the Prince, who was in his own palace with his family.

Vessantara, fearing that something had happened to his parents, asked anxiously about their health. But the poor old minister could not speak, as he was choked with tears, and he only shook his head in answer to the anxious questions of the Prince.

At last he recovered his self-possession and said sadly: "In spite of the Royal wish the Cibis demand that you should be banished from the kingdom."

"What have I done?" exclaimed the Prince in astonishment. "I have not left the Path of Righteousness. I have not neglected my duties. Why should the Cibis be angry with me?"

The minister answered: "They cannot understand your lofty spirit of charity. Your feelings were pure when you gave that most splendid of elephants away to the covetous Brahmanas; but the Cibis are furious with you and they say that a prince, who cannot discriminate between wise and unwise charity, ought not to become the ruler of the country, but should rather become an Ascetic."

The Prince answered gently: "The Cibis do not understand me, I see. They only see the outside seeming foolishness of my deed. They could not understand either, that I would give away my eyes or even my head, if it were for the good of another creature. Even if the Cibis banish me or kill me, they will not keep me back from giving in charity. I am ready to go to the Penance-Grove on Mount Vanka."

The old minister, bowing low before the saintly Prince, left him with tears in his eyes and told king Sandumaha that his son was quite ready to obey his orders.

After the messenger of woe had left the Palace, Prince Vessantara turned to his faithful wife Mantridevi and said: "You have heard what has happened. Put together all my fortune with yours—I need no wealth now. Give charity to everyone who deserves it, and speak kind words of advice to the one who receives from your hands. Charity done thus is imperishable. Be dutiful to my parents, and a good mother to our children."

Mantri was almost broken-hearted when she heard this; but she gathered all her strength together and said with outward calm: "My Lord, where you go, there I go also. Attending to you, I shall not mind death, but to live without you would be worse than death."

"Is that really thy mind, my Princess?" asked Prince Vessantara.

Mantri, seeing that her husband was wavering about going alone to the forest, answered joyously: "I love the forest as you do: I love to hear the birds singing in the branches of the overhanging trees; I love to see the deer peeping without fear through the bushes. Then see how glad you will be to see our dear children decorated with wreaths of wild flowers which they will gather, playing in the grass round the Penance-Grove. There, far away from wicked people, we will live happy and content, though alone. Our hut made of leaves, near the laughing brook and the moonlit rocks at night, will be far better than our palace, surrounded by artificial gardens."

Hearing these eloquent words, looking at the pleading face of his beloved wife, the Prince consented to take his wife and children with him.

Now they arranged that the beggars should be fed in their absence and that their attendants should be cared for. Then they prepared themselves for leaving the palace and the capital in the early morning.

In the palace of the King there was great distress and also the poor, the sick and the lowly people grieved. They could not understand that a Prince like Vessantara, whom they called the "Fruit-Tree," the "Foster child of Mother Earth" could be banished from the realm. They said: "The Guardians of the Four Quarters of the Earth must be absent from their posts, otherwise they would not allow this 'Well of Pure Waters of Wisdom' to be made useless. Righteousness is either asleep or dead," they cried. "How can we live when our 'Well of Plenty' is empty?"

Prince Vessantara heard the cry of the poor and he opened his treasury and gave all his wealth away to the poor and needy. His jewels, his gold, his silver, his clothes, his grains, his oxen, his carriages—all were distributed among the poor with a cheerful face and with kind teachings. And when all was gone, he took leave of his grieving parents. With his wife and children he mounted his chariot, his last possession, and drove out of the city, followed for quite a distance by a crowd of grateful people, who had been enriched by his charity. He drove with a contented heart away from his beloved city with its poor, who sent blessings after him.

While nearing a forest, some Brahmanas met him, and they begged from him the four horses, which were drawing his chariot.

Vessantara got down from his chariot and gave the horses to the begging Brahmanas and began to pull the chariot himself. But the Devas came to his rescue. Four Yakshas in the forms of red deer appeared and they drew the chariot.

The Prince, full of joy said to the Princess: "See Mantri, the Asceties of the Penance-Grove are so kind to all creatures, that these deer have come to honour us as new guests in this way."

"I rather believe" answered Mantri " that it is your super-human practice of charity, which has brought these deer to you to repay the debts of some creature helped by you."

Now Vessantara came to the woods with his family, and here a Brahman met him and he asked him for his chariot. The Prince did not refuse this request either. He got down with his wife and children and the Brahman took the chariot away.

The Prince now took his little son on his arm and Mantri carried her little daughter and thus they wandered on. The fruit-trees reached down their branches to them, so that they could easily pluck the fruits, inviting them like hospitable friends to be their guests. The sweetly rippling brooks refreshed their thirty lips. So the difficult wandering became a refreshing walk to them, for balmy breezes were blowing and the roads seemed smooth as a bed of flowers.

At last they saw Mount Vanka before them and on it stood a simple hut of leaves just ready for their reception. It was made for them by Visvakarma, the architect of the Devas, ordered by Sakra himself.

The Grove called Penance-Grove was surrounded by flowers, fruit-trees and flowering bushes. Birds sang on the branches of the trees and peacocks strutted about, while large-eyed deer peeped through the bushes. A river, like a girdle of pure blue water, encircled it, making of it an island, and a fresh breeze greeted them, laden with sweet-smelling flower-dust.

Vessantara with his wife and their two children took possession of the Grove in joyful happiness. There, for six months they lived in content. Vessantara doing penance, but enjoying the company of his family and having sweet talks with his children, who liked the forest-life very much.

Mantri was always busy attending to their wants. One day, she had gone into the jungle to search for edible roots and to pluck fruits.

The Prince was in the hermitage taking care of the children, who were playing under the trees of the Grove, when a travel-stained Brahman arrived. He seemed old and cross and his dust-covered feet showed that he had been walking for a long time. He seemed poor also, for his clothes were ragged.

The Prince rejoiced to see a mendicant coming to his humble door, and he met him with kind words, inviting him into the hermitage to rest and eat. Then he asked the

Brahman what boon he craved from him.

The Brahman, who had been sent by his old wife to the Bodhisattva, and who was thinking of her demand, said bluntly and roughly: "I would not dare ask any boon from anybody but you whose fame, gained by charity, has spread everywhere. I heard that you had given away everything but your wife and children, and as my wife needs help in her old age, I demand from you, as my boon, your two children to attend to her as servants."

Like a stab from a knife these words penetrated the heart of the Bodhisattva; but thinking of his vow not to refuse any gift which he could give, he answered calmly: "Even my two darling children I will give to thee, as thou demandest."

The Brahman uttered a short blessing and said: "I want to take the children away at once, for fear that you will repent of your promise."

The children, who had heard what their father said, pleaded to see their mother first and bid her good-bye before they departed.

The father's heart was moved by love and compassion and he said to the Brahman: "Rest here for the night and to morrow morning the children, who are thine now, will go with thee after bidding farewell to their mother."

The Brahman answered: "I fear that your wife will prevent my taking her children away, for she is a woman and women are usually hindrances to their husbands."

"My wife is a real helpmate," answered the Prince "and she will not go against my wishes. Besides she is at one with me in the point of charity; so do not fear! Only think how young and weak my children are, not accustomed to any work; what can they do? Take them to my father, King Sandumaha, of the Cibis and when he sees how his grandchildren have come into your hands as slaves, he will redeem them and make you rich and you can get servants to attend on you and your wife."

"No," said the Brahman sharply, "I shall not go near your father the King, because he will think that I have stolen them and he will punish me. I want these children to attend to my wife and I want them at once."

Then the Bodhisattva took the water-pot and poured the water of giving over the greedily outstretched hands of the Brahman, whilst his tears mingled with the water.

The Brahman, glad of his success, muttered a short blessing and called the children harshly to come with him.

The poor little children fell on their knees, embraced the legs of their father and pleaded with tears in their eyes to be allowed to wait till their mother came.

But the heart of the Brahman was not moved. He tied their hands together with a creeper and he forced them to go with him.

The little girl, Krishnajina, complained that the tie was hurting her wrists and she exclaimed. "Surely this is no Brahman, because the Brahmans are said to be righteous. This must be a Yaksha, who wants to eat us. Oh, what will mother say, when she finds us gone?"

The cruel old Brahman only shouted at her to stop her wailings and urged her on.

The boy, Jalia, did not mind the tied hands, but he said: "Our poor mother will weep for us for a long time. Father, give her our last farewells, for I doubt whether we shall see her again." Then turning to his sister he said sweetly: "Come sister, let us die together, for what is the use of life, now that father has given us away to a Brahman, who wants money." With these words the poor children followed the cruel Brahman, who was urging them on with hard words.

The Bodhisattva heard these pitiful words and he was almost stunned with grief. However he felt he must not repent of his deed, but remember his vow. And so he sat down on his kusagrass couch and the pity for his children overcame him and he exclaimed "How could this Brahman take my children who are not accustomed to any work? How will they stand the walking with their tender naked feet? Who will give them food and drink, when they are hungry and thirsty? These thoughts almost kill me, how will my poor children stand it who have been brought up in ease and comfort? The separation from my children burns like fire in me : but still, he who walks on the Path of Righteousness must not repent of what he has done, and so I must cease lamenting."

In the meanwhile, Princess Mantridevi was searching for fruits and roots in the jungle and because her mind was uneasy with the fear of some coming trouble, she hastened home, fearing that something had happened to her children, whom she had left in her husband's care, playing under the trees.

On her way to the grove she met some wild animals who tried to hinder her quick steps. They did not harm her, but they lingered round her and looked at her with pitying eyes. What did they mean ?

At last she came near the hut and she hoped to hear the joyous cries of her children for they used to run to meet her at her call. But this day all was quiet, no voices greeted her, no answer came to her sweet call of "Jalia, Krishnajina !" Were they asleep, tired after their happy play ? She hurried on to the hermitage, put the gathered fruits and roots and herbs down and rushed to the hut. Here also all was silent, no children to be seen.

And there on the grass-couch sat her husband, silent and grave, seemingly bowed down by grief! What did it all mean ? "Where are our children ?" she called out anxiously, looking pleadingly at the Prince.

The Prince could not speak for woe and the poor mother in anguish after three times questioning and not getting an answer, rushed out again into the jungle for her children. Here she searched all the places, where she hoped she might find them. She even imagined she heard their voices, sweet as the voices of the Devis.

"Oh my children, my children," she wailed, "my lotus-buds brought up as tender flowers, not accustomed to anything but happiness. Where are you? Has any animal frightened you away from your play and are you lost in the jungle now? Hear my voice, my sweet ones, come to me. Listen to my cries, ye animals of the forest, tell me ye birds and ye insects, ye flowers and ye bushes where are my children? Have ye not seen them? Oh help me find them. Tell me, speak to me ye, who understand my words."

The animals gathered round her, they looked at her with pitying eyes, but they were silent, they dared not tell her what they had seen. They dared not tell her that they saw an old man driving them in haste through that jungle, with harsh words and with cruel blows! Oh the pity of it! Only the parrots, the crows and the minas seemed to nod and say: "There, there they went."

"Where, where?" the poor mother cried, "my eyes are blind from weeping my heart will turn into a stone, if I do not find my children." The birds could not speak for sorrow and the poor mother fell down exhausted, surrounded by the pitying animals, and lay unconscious throughout the night.

When she awoke, she dragged herself back to the hut, where she found the Bodhisattva in the same silent mood. She threw herself before him on the ground and implored him with outstretched hands to speak, to tell her even the worst. "All the animals are silent, and now you too do not speak. Where are my children? My heart will break if I do not get an answer," and she fell down as if dead.

Now the Bodhisattva roused himself. He sprinkled water on her, and, when at last she revived, when her eyes looked in agony at him, then he told her the whole sad story and explained to her that it had been impossible for him to tell her what almost broke his heart: "Share with me that merit of this greatest of gifts to the poor old Brahman," he said.

Then she shared with him and resolved that, even if he were to give her away, she would not complain. Thus these two saintly persons sat in silence for a long time and their prayers for the welfare of their beloved children rose like a holy pure pink vapour up to the throne of Sakra, who looked down in awe and wonder at the silent human beings in the hut of the Penance-Grove on Mount Vanka.

At last Princess Mantridevi roused herself, bowed down lowly before the Bodhisattva and said: "I hear hymns of praise sung to you by heavenly beings, I feel the earth trembling with joy and see golden flowers, like bright lightnings showering down on you. Therefore grieve no more, you have again become the tree that gives its fruits and the well that gives its waters for the benefit of all creatures, as you were before when you lived as the happy Prince of Jayatura."

So spoke in admiration the faithful wife of Prince Vessantara, and both, though bowed down with grief for the loss of their children, did not repent of the deed of mercy. And the Gods rejoiced and were amazed, when the Guardians of the Quarters of the Earth reported what they had seen.

And Sakra in his exaltation cried: "Hail to the coming Buddha, who can sacrifice his children. Will he be willing to give away his wife also? I shall test him:—" So the following morning, when the sad Prince Vessantara and his faithful wife Mantridevi were talking together quietly, Sakra appeared before them as a Brahman coming to them for a gift. Hospitality and kind words were offered to him. When the question of the boon which he desired came, this Brahmin without hesitation said: "Yesterday you gave away your two children and to-day I want your wife, who looks like a Goddess."

The Bodhisattva looked at the Brahman and looked at his wife. She stood there like a statue as though stunned by a blow; but no sound of woe came from her lips Then the Bodhisattva took the water pot with his right hand and with his left the hand of the faithful

Mantridevi and poured the water of donation over her hand and on the hand of the Brahman, while tears of deep grief mingled with the water.

No anger was in the heart of Mantridevi, for she knew the Bodhisattva's mind. No complaint crossed her lips, but unspeakable woe stood written in her face for having to leave the one she loved.

Then Sakra in admiration exclaimed: "Only those whose hearts are purified would understand and believe this wonder! Obeying his vow of unattachment he gives up his dear children and even his beloved wife! Surely Thy glory, O Great One, will make the glory of the Gods disappear, as the sunlight makes the stars disappear from the sky. Truly the Yakshas, the Gandharvas, the Devas, including Sakra and all human beings, must bow to Thee in adoration."

Then Sakra assumed his brilliant shape as the King of the Devas and said to the Bodhisattva: "The moonshine must stay with the moon, and so I give back to Thee Thy virtuous wife, Mantridevi. Do not grieve about Thy children any more. Soon Thy father will come, accompanied by Thy children and all of you will be together again in the home of Thy father."

After saying these words the King of the Devas disappeared.

And Sakra's words came true. The cruel old Brahman was forced by the power of

Sakra to take the children of Vessantara to the land of Parah Sandumah, where the old king heard of the sacrifice which his son had performed in giving away his children. His heart melted in him, when he saw his grand-children as slaves of the Brahman. He redeemed them, by giving to the Brahman their weight in gold and he came with his Queen and the children to the Penance-Grove on Mount Vanka and took Prince Vessantara and his faithful wife Mantridevi back to his own country, where the people humbly asked forgiveness for the misunderstanding of the wonderful Prince Vessantara, who had been willing to give up wife and children for the sake of charity.

Prince Vessantara reigned long after his father's death, to the benefit of his faithful subjects, who adored him and never misunderstood him again in his boundless charity to all mankind.

PART II.

THE STORY OF PRINCE SIDDHARTHA. THE LAST BIRTH ON EARTH OF THE BODHISATTVA.

The Bodhisattva rested in the Tushita Heaven [10] among the Gods and waited for the last birth which he had to undergo on Earth. In this last birth he was to reach Buddhahood.

In the World below, the time was getting ripe when another Great Teacher was to appear and the five signs [11] of the coming birth of a Buddha became visible.

The Devas saw them and proclaimed that the Bodhisattva must be incarnated for the last time, to teach the world and become a Buddha.

After being informed of this, the Bodhisattva went to the Temple Dharmachchāya and, sitting on his lion-throne Saddharma, preached the Law to the Gods of the Tushita Heaven.

Some of the sons of the Gods left their heaven, came down to earth in the shape of Brahmanas and preached to the Pratyeka

Buddhas[12] on earth, that in twelve years the Bodhisattva would come down to earth to become the Buddha, and so the mission of these minor teachers would end.

The Bodhisattva, looking down from the Tushita Heaven, searched among the people of the earth to find the purest and best family in which he could take birth. He discovered near the snows of the great Himalayas a King of the Sakyas[13] who reigned in Kapilavastu,[14] the river Rohini[15] watering its borders.

Pure was his descent and he possessed immense riches. His name was Suddhodana. His girl-wife, Maya-Devi, was equally pure in descent, the daughter of the Sakya-Prince Suprabuddha. Sweet and pure was Maya-Devi, like a Virgin of the Gods, free from woman's tricks and always speaking the truth. Beautiful she was to look at, with golden skin and eyes as blue as the blue lotus-flower. Maya was her name and a Queen of magic fantasy she looked in her innocent and radiant beauty.

This was to be the earthly Mother of the future Buddha.

I.

MAYA'S DREAM

There were great rejoicings in the Palace of King Suddhodana, in Kapilavastu, in Jambudwipa; for wonderful signs occurred which

made everybody believe in the coming of something great.

The sages of the land prophesied to the King that a wonderful son was to be born to him. And yet Maya the Queen, was chaste and pure, and not yet united to the King.

She had pleaded with him, whom she loved and revered, to remain a virgin and he, seeing heavenly light in her lotus-eyes, had bent his knee before her in reverence and let her have her own way.

And what were the earthly signs which made the King, the Queen and the people wonder? Hear, ye, who desire to hear!

All plants in the palace-gardens became full of buds, although the right time of flowering had not come. All impurities left the palace.

Many sweet singing birds came from the Himalayas out of season to the palace roofs, and settled there singing sweet songs.

All fruits in the gardens ripened at the same time.

The lotus-ponds filled with sweet lotuses all in full bloom and larger than ever before.

The provisions in the King's granaries did not diminish, although they were being used as always.

The musical instruments in the women's palace played without being touched by human hand.

And when the fullmoon-day of Essela-Massa (July) came, soft radiance shone like a halo over the roof of e Queen's chamber.

Have all the jewels left their caskets and are they pouring fourth their lustre to illuminate Queen Maya's dream ?

Balmy breezes were blowing during the fullmoon night of Essela. The silvery palm leaves moved gently, as if their beauty had to be enhanced, for Queen Maya had a wonderful dream.

Peacefully lying on her stately couch in her own chamber, watched by her faithful women, Queen Maya dreamed.

She dreamed shat she was wrapped in a cloud of holy light, when the roof of her chamber seemed to open and the four Deva-Rajahs* appeared.

They took Queen Maya witn the couch on which she slept and carried her to the Anotata Lake in the Himalayas,† where she was bathed by the Devis of the Deva-Rajahs of the Four Quarters of the Earth, in order to remove all human stain from her. Then she was clothed with divine garments and annointod with divine oil.

The Deva-Rajuhs returned and took Queen Maha-Maya to the Deva-Vimāna

---

* The Deva-Rajahs are the Guardians of the four quarters of the Earth.

† The Anotâta Lake is a mysterious Lake in the Himalayas in which it is said only Buddhas, Arahats, and Devas are allowed to bathe. Its water is perfectly pure. It is surrounded by five rocks which protect it against the direct rays of the sun One of the streams which rises from this Lake is the Ganges and therefore it is called the holy river.—

Maya's Dream

(Palace in Deva-Land. Then, in her dream, she saw the roof of the chamber where she rested, lift, and standing on four white lotus-flowers and bathed in silvery light, a snow white elephant descended. He walked thrice round the cough of Queen Maha-Maya, from left to right, and handed her a snow-white lotus flower. She, the room in which she slept, and then the whole world was filled with radiance, while a far away voice whispered :—"Hear! all ye who have ears to hear! Rise, ye who have fallen! for the Buddha has come to earth to preach to you again." Slowly the radiance faded away, the White Elephant ascended again and Queen Maha-Maya awoke! Such happiness was hers, that she thought the whole world must feel it also.

At once she arose and made her faithful servants dress her and decorte her with flowers and jewels. Thus she went to the Asoka Grove near her palace with her women and sent word to King Suddhodana to come at once to visit her.

The whole air seemed full of song and happiness, and in awe and reverence the King bowed before his Queen, seeing her look so fair and holy.

Maya told him her dream and asked him to send for those who are learned in the Vedas and Upanishads to explain the meaning of her dream.

And lo! the Wise-ones have only one one explanation! Thy answer:

"Hail O Queen of Heaven! Hail O King of the Sakyas! Maya will be the mother of the holy Buddha, who always comes in the shape of a white elephant to announce his birth on earth."

II.

THE BIRTH OF THE PRINCE

King Suddhodana believed in the signs that his immaculate wife should become the mother of a holy child, and he had a palace built for her where she could live alone, surrounded only by her friends and trusty servants, awaiting the birth of her child.

Queen Maya was very happy. She was ever busily thinking of the poor and helping them in every way she could. She gave away what she could spare of her bounty and the poor and afflicted blessed her. Her hand healed the sick in body and her words those whose minds were troubled.

King Suddhodana himself prepared also for the reception of the Holy-One, by living the life of a Brahmacharya[16] and so the time went on.

In the palace-garden in Kapilavastu wondrous buds of flowers appeared, all out of season, and in the palace of the women mines of gems were found. Lovely, balmy breezes blew everywhere and sweet low music, played on invisible vinas,* filled the air. What did all

* A vina is a stringed instrument resembling a guitar.

Queen Maya goes to Lumbini Gardens.

this mean? It indicated that the time had come when, to the joy of all people, the future Lord of Heaven and Earth was to be born.

It was ten months after Queen Maya's dream and now she felt that her time had come.

She asked to be taken to the pleasure-garden Lumbini, which had been laid out for her own mother by her father, Suprabuddha.

Here she walked among the flowers. When she came to a Sal-tree in a grove, the tree bent down one large branch to make a bower for her, and Maya took hold of it with her right hand, which shone like a bright stream of light. Flowers showered down from the tree on her, although it was not the time of blossoms, and made a perfumed couch for the Mother of the Lord.

And here in this fragrant bower the Prince was born, received by the Devas from heaven, who would not allow human hands to touch Him.

When he was born he was not like any other babe. He stood like a herald, himself announcing the coming of the future Lord.

The child [17] made seven steps towards the East, and where his feet had rested seven lotuses sprang up, white as the snow from the Himalayas, and he said: "I shall be the first in all good deeds, the source of all good!" He turned to the South and exclaimed: "I am worthy to be honoured by Gods and men."

To the West he made seven steps and spoke: "I am the noblest on earth. This is my last birth, I shall destroy birth and decay, death and pain." Towards the North he turned and whispered: "I shall be without successor among all creatures." Then looking down to earth he said solemnly. "I shall destroy the Evil-One and his army. I shall send the rain of the great Religion into the depth of Hell, and destroy there the fire even in the deepest regions, so that Peace shall reign." Then looking up to Heaven he said: "On me all look that dwell there above."

So He stood, announcing his own advent, enveloped in the brilliant halo of his future Buddhahood, and only his earthly mother, Maya, knew the meaning of all this wonder.

And the Heavens seemed to open and glad hymns of praise sounded from above. The earth shook in acknowledgment of the miracle that happened and gladness spread over the world.

The news of the birth of a Prince came to the palace, and, as was the custom, a golden palanquin was brought to fetch him home with his mother.

Who were the bearers, who eagerly had taken hold of the four poles of the palanquin, you ask? The Four Regents of the Earth, from the East, South, West and North.

Hearing the clarion call of the future Buddha, they had come down from their heavenly posts and in the shape of bearers, carried the wondrous burden to the palace. An invisible procession of the Devas followed and thus the future Buddha, now a small babe, in his mother's arms, entered his earthly palace where the flowers in the gardens were in full bloom. All buds had opened to receive the Lord.

King Suddhodana grew uneasy and did not know what all this meant. For besides all the wonders that occurred, many pilgrims had come with gifts of cloth and jewels and honey and spices.

He asked the Wise Ones and they said that nothing but good would come, for seven signs [18] accompanied the birth of the child. They explained that once in a thousand years such a Prince is born, a Master, who would rule the world. And so the Prince was called Siddhartha, (All-prospering.)

King Suddhodana in his gladness fed the hungry and gave riches to the poor, and all Kapilavastu was in festive array and music and feasting filled the city.

Up in the Himalaya Mountains, under his peepul-tree there prayed Asita, an old hermit, wise and pious. He was dead to the world's pleasures. His mind was bent only on spiritual things. Deep in his meditation, he heard the Devas sing the praises of the new-born Prince and he said to his adopted son Naradatta: "Let us hasten to Kapilavastu, where the Lord is born."

Arrived at the palace, they laid down the Argha[19] sacrifice at the feet of the babe, fell down at his feet and worshipoed him with joined hands.

Then the old Asita got up, walked three times round the child, took him in his arms and contemplated the thirty-two signs of Buddhahood[20] visible to his opened inner sight. Solemnly he said : "If he will remain and govern his realm, he will become a most powerful sovereign. But if he leaves the world, he will become the Tathāgata, a perfect Buddha. Alas, that my old eyes will not see Him as the Buddha," and tears fell down over his withered cheeks. "But still I die in peace, for my eyes have seen the Lord."

After a few moments Asita continued : "Happy thy house, O King ! where such a blossom has come forth, that only blooms once in a thousand years. Yet not entirely happy canst thou be, O King, for a sword will pierce thy heart, who lovest thy sweet Queen. She is too sacred to bear another child. She will join the Devis seven days after having given to thee this wondrous child."

And so it happened. After seven days Queen Maya-Devi left this earth. Sweetly falling asleep, she did not wake again on earth, but was awakened in heaven where she reigns in perfect bliss.

III.

PRINCE SIDDHARTHA

A foster-mother was found for Prince Siddhartha in Queen Maya's sister Princess Prajapati, who nursed and loved him like a mother.

The Prince grew up a lovely boy. He was always kind and courteous, gentle and loving and it was soon seen that he had the wish to learn and the capacity to understand.

His first entrance into the Temple, where the wise Viswamitra was to teach him, was accompanied by wonders ; for behold the lifeless statues of the Gods came down from their pedestals and fell at his feet, so the Lalitavishtara says.

Viswamitra himself, almost overcome with the splendour that shone from the person of the little prince, found out soon that his pupil could write almost as well as he could, on his little slate of sandalwood covered with emery powder. In arithmetic he even knew more than his teacher, and in every science and art he soon outshone him. Viswamitra spoke in admiration : "Thou art the teacher of the teachers. Thou art Guru, not I. Thou hast come to me to show me that thou knowest all. I reverence thee, I worship thee, sweet Prince."

Thus Prince Siddhartha grew up, scholarly, deeply thoughtful, but also bold on horseback and in games of war. He drove the chariot skilfully, he could shoot well with his bow and arrows; but always he loved books better than anything else and often he used to leave his companions to sit under a tree, to muse and meditate, to the wonder of his cousin Dewadatta, who loved sport better than learning.

One day King Suddhodana went to a spring festival and he took Prince Siddhartha with him. The young prince enjoyed seeing the oxen plough the fields, the peasant joyfully walking behind the plough, and to him the regularly turned up soil looked like a rippling sea. He loved to see and hear the gurgling waters of the springs under the palm trees. He enjoyed listening to the songs of the jungle birds and the cooing of the wood-doves and he observed even the lizards nodding solemnly and enjoying the spring-time. How happy was the world, he thought. But then he heard a cry of pain. A hawk had caught a small bird and carried it off to its nest. His wistful eye was further opened and the young boy saw how the stronger was feeding on the weaker, the snake on the lizard, the lizard on the worm, the bird on the fish and so on. Then sadness began to fill his youthful heart and he wished he could help the weak ones.

There stood a jambu-tree among the other trees near the field where his father the king had gone to witness the harvest festival. There the young prince sat down to think. Long did he sit there, quite alone, absorbed in his deep thoughts. When he was found there sometime after the midday-sun had sent his rays straight down upon the tree under which he sat, the shadow of the jambu-tree had not changed and the little prince sat yet in the shade.

When this was reported to King Suddhodana he wondered, and the prophecy of Asita came back to his mind, and he bowed down low to his little son, while a mysterious small voice whispered in the tree. "As long as the shadow lies on the prince's heart, my shadow shall not move."

Another incident is related in the young prince's life, which shows his great compassion for all creatures.

Once he was sitting in his garden in deep thought, as many a time before, when a flock of silver white swans flew over the garden, on their way to the Himalayas. Devadatta, the prince's cousin, who was ever ready with his bow and arrow to show his skilfulness in shooting, aimed at the leading swan and shot through its wing. It fell down bleeding among the bushes. Siddhartha heard the fall and, running to the rescue of the wounded swan, lifted it up, put it on his knee and soothed the frightened bird.

The little prince caressed and spoke to it and drew the cruel arrow from its quivering wing. He stopped the rushing blood with his gentle hand and nursed the bird back to life, putting cooling leaves and honey on the bleeding wound. Curious himself how it must feel when hurt by an arrow, he pressed the sharp point into his own wrist. Then he turned back to the swan to cure it, with compassion in his heart. Thus he was found by the attendants of prince Devadatta, who asked him for the swan which their master had shot.

But Prince Siddhartha, laying his smooth check against the white swan's neck said: "Tell my cousin that the swan is not dead, but that I nursed it back to life, and therefore the swan is mine, as I rescued it. This swan is the first of many things that shall be mine by the right of mercy and love. If he is not satisfied, let this matter be brought before the King and be decided by the Wise Ones."

And this was done and it was decided that the rescuer of life had the right to keep the bird, not the one who tried to destroy its life.

So Prince Siddhartha began his life of mercy.

IV.

PRINCE SIDDHARTHA'S MARRIAGE'

Prince Siddhartha had grown to his 19th year and he was a noble youth. His figure was slender and straight, his eyes seemed to look deep into the future. The movements of his limbs were graceful and yet strong. His habits were those of a thinker : but still, when called upon, he would show his skill in shooting, riding and those physical feats which delight a young warrior.

The Wise Ones said to King Suddhodana : "Now the time has come that Prince Siddhartha must marry. The seven jewels[21] which a sovereign should possess are his. Either he will become the sovereign of the world or the Tathāgata, the sovereign of the heavens."

King Suddhodana, in his heart of hearts, wished his beloved son to become his heir and successor on the throne, so that he should leave his realm in the hands of him whom he loved best. He spoke to his son of marriage and of his own happiness in knowing that after the flames of his funeral pyre had died down, his son would hold the reins of government.

Long mused the Prince on the words of his father, the King, and then he said: "If I should want to wed, my father, my bride must possess all the qualities which ought to adorn a woman. She must be pure and beautiful as my mother was. If thou canst find me one like her, my father, then I shall obey thy command."

So the King announced by beat of drum that all sweet maids of Kapilavastu and the surrounding country should come to a festival where Prince Siddhartha should give out prizes to all, and to the fairest the best prize would be given.

Many sweet maids came, arrayed in their prettiest saris, with blossoms in their deep raven hair and the bright tilaka[22] between their shining eyes.

Prince Siddhartha was seated on his throne, and all these lovely Indian girls passed before him, shyly looking down and each receiving a gift from him. Some got a gay sari, some a jewel, others a necklace or a bracelet. But the young Prince sat quiet and solemn, and no welcome smile shone on his face.

All seemed to have passed by and he leaned back wearily on his soft cushions. Then a sweet voice said: "Is there a gift left for me—the last of all?"

Prince Siddhartha starts, he looks down and meets the upturned eyes of Yasodhara, the daughter of King Suprabuddha, his own cousin. Yes, these eyes he knows, a picture of a past life comes before his inner sight: "A hunter's son, playing with some forest girls, whom he decorates. But the last of all he makes happy in giving her a tame fawn and she is the one whom he loves."

Prince Siddhartha takes an emerald ring from his finger and hands it to her with a gracious bow and says: "Wear it for my sake, princess." She bows and leaves, but both know that their lot will be one, as it has been before, in former lives.

The king's attendants had seen the start, the smile and the gift of the princely ring, and King Suddhodana announced his wishes to Yasodhara's father, accompanied with rich gifts.

"I cannot give my daughter Yasodhara, the jewel of my household to a dreamer and a book-worm." That was King Suprabuddha's answer to King Suddhodana. "My daughter must be wed by a strong prince, who can defend her and protect her."

When Prince Siddhartha heard this, he only smiled and said: "My father, let a festival be held in seven days and let it be proclaimed that all the valiant princes are invited to show their skill in war games, but also in the war of words. Let it be understood that the one who will be the conqueror in both shall receive the Princess Yasodhara as the prize."

"Be it so, my son," answered the old king. Now preparations were made in Kapilavastu for a great festival, and all the brave young princes, Devadatta included, came together, all bent on winning such a prize.

When the seven days of preparation were over, there was such a display of banners and flags and flowers, and such a blast of conch shells, that all the valour and all the beauty of India seemed gathered together in Kapilavastu. And in a palanquin of gold, arrayed as a bride, with shining eyes, which gleamed through the thin clouds of her veil, Yasodhara arrived, the prize of him who would gain her by his strength.

Would he win, the one whose ring she wore? There he stood alone, beautiful and strong, seemingly looking into the future with his dark eyes. One glance only he cast upon her and she knew that he would win, and content and happy she sat down, her veil deep drawn so that no other eye should look at her.

The war-play began. Devadatta, the champion in archery commenced, and he shot well. When Siddhartha's turn came he surpassed them all and a joyful conch-shell blast announced him as the victor. He had scored over them all and that with the old bow that no one could string, that had been given to an ancestor of his and which had been kept in the Temple from olden times.

Then came the game with swords. Who will win this? Devadatta, Nanda, Arjuna, all cut through the Tala-trees with one clean stroke. And Siddhartha? He saw two sister-trees and with one stroke he cut them both. They yet stood erect and Devadatta cried: "He missed, he missed," and believed Siddhartha conquered. But there came a sudden wind and the two tree-tops crashed to earth and showed a clean cut through them both. Yasodhara had lifted her black and gold veil to see and only dropped it when again the conch-shell sounded the blast of victory for Siddhartha.

Now the race began. All the Princess were on well-bred steeds of strength and fire. Siddhartha rode his white Kantaka, his wonderful war-horse. Again the victory was his, for Kantaka was best of all. But the young Princes cried: "That is not fair, for anyone must win on such a horse as Kantaka. Let us mount an unbroken horse and see who can ride the best."

A young stallion was brought, as black as night. Never had a rider sat on his back. His eyes looked fierce. With chains he was bound. All the Sakya Princes tried to jump on his back; but he snorted, fumed and reared and all had to kiss the dust in shame. Only Arjuna, the tamer of wild horses, could keep his seat a little while and he thought he had won. But then the wild steed turned its head and gripping the rider's foot with its teeth, threw him into the sand: "Let me try him" cried Siddhartha. He put his hand gently over the horse's eyes, whispered a kind word into its ears, and stroked the proud neck. Then he mounted the wild horse and rode three times round the circle.

Thrice sounds the conch-shell and King Suprabuddha and the princes cry : "The war is over. Prince Siddhartha wins in all. He only can get the prize."

Lovingly King Suprabuddha took the hand of Prince Siddhartha and said : "Who would have thought that thou, brought up among the rose bowers of thy father's palace-gardens, couldst with all thy wisdom also be the bravest and strongest of all? Take the sweet prize, my lovely daughter, and be her guide, her protector and her loving Lord."

Hand in hand they walked through the prostrate crowd, Yasodhara with bowed head but sweet smiling face, hidden again under the black and gold veil.

Prince Siddhartha looking at her in her youth and beauty had another vision and he whispered to her : "Didst thou know, my princess, that once, long ago, I won thee as a tiger, amongst all the other tigers? That veil of thine, in black and gold, does show me that thou also dost remember." She only nodded and understood.

They were married with great joy and many festivities. Their hands were tied, as was the custom, and the wedding-cake was broken. The rice and rose water were thrown on them and thrice they walked round the lighted household fire. Gifts were bestowed freely on

Brahmanas, and King Suprabuddha gave, with loving heart and in complete confidence, his daughter Yasodhara into the care of Prince Siddhartha.

V.

THE RENUNCIATION

Prince Siddhartha and Princess Yasodhara lived surrounded only by love and beauty. Splendid palaces had been built for the prince, one for the spring, one for the hot season, and one for monsoon time. But now another palace was added and it was called Vishram van and it was said to be more beautiful than even the palace of the Gods. Here old King Suddhodana hoped that his son, living together with his lovely wife, would forget all thoughts of leaving his home with its splendours to become a World-Teacher; for again and again the prophecy of Asita came back to his mind.

Besides, the old king had a dream in which he saw Siddhartha leaving the palace, clad in a monk's robe; and this so troubled him that he ordered a strong wall to be built round the wide gardens, with three gates. Before each gate a strong watch was set. The outer door was so heavy that only a hundred men could open it. And it was ordered, on pain of death, that the prince was not to be allowed to pass through any of the gates without the King's permission. By this means King Suddhodana hoped to prevent the knowledge of the struggle for lifet in he outside world from reaching the young prince. It was also ordered that, whenever sickness should break out among the lovely crowd of serving, dancing and singing girls in the palace, the suffering one should be quietly removed out of sight. And so for a time Siddhartha, ignorant of the struggles and sorrows of the outside world, lived in happiness and joy with his sweet wife Yasodhara, who was in herself a wonder of loveliness, purity and grace.

When a son was born to them King Suddhodana was doubly happy, for he thought that now Siddhartha would have no longing to wander beyond the gates. The old King mused; "I can now die in peace, for my kingdom will be in the hands of my great son, the most perfect of princes living. My son will surely not leave his son and wife and his kingdom."

And Prince Siddhartha? Yes, he was happy. He loved his wife and son. But still in midnight musings and in dreams it came to him to ask: "Can *all* be happiness in life? Is everyone as gay and glad as we? I must go out into the world to see!" and he resolved to go out of his prison-house of love, to see his capital Kapilavastu.

When King Suddhodana heard that resolve

he sent out criers all around to order that all the roads to Kapilavastu and the city itself hould be decorated and no persons old or sick should show themselves. No funeral-pyres should be erected that day till Prince Siddharta had returned to his palace.

The women decorated themselves and their houses, strewed flowers before their doors, and hung the trees with flags. The temples were newly adorned and the town looked like a flower-garden. Men, women and children attired in their festive garments awaited with eager faces the coming of their future Lord. When Prince Siddhartha came on his chariot, which was guided by his faithful charioteer Channa and all hailed him as future King, he felt quite happy, thinking how fair the world was, almost as beautiful as his own small realm with wife and child, flowers, fountains, singing and dancing girls, and tame deer. "Drive on, Channa," he cried, "I want to see more of this beautiful world which I did not know before. How easy it is to make people happy, if they who serve and toil for me are glad when they only see me! Why should I stay away from them? Drive on, my faithful Channa!"

But there, outside the city's Eastern gate, what was the sight that came before the prince's eyes? It was a poor old tottering man who did not know the decree of the King. He held on feebly to his crutch and when he saw the princely chariot he stretched out his thin, trembling hand and asked for alms with anguish in his eyes, "Go away quickly!" cried the crowd. "The Prince! the Prince! he must not see you. That is the will of the king!"

But Prince Siddhartha had seen the old man, and he called out: "Give him alms, Channa! Help him, ye people, for he seems weak." Then he turned to Channa and said: "O Channa, take me back home. I never saw so sad a sight! Must all of us become as he is when we are old? Is such the life of human kind, the life that I thought fair?"

The impression which this sight had made an Prince Siddhartha was lasting and he would muse and dream, and not even sweet Yasodhara could brush away the thoughts that made his brow look dark.

That night King Suddhodana had seven troubled dreams. One of them, that troubled him most, was that he thought he saw a tower rise higher and higher, till it reached the clouds. Then appeared on the highest terrace the figure of Prince Siddhartha. With wide outstretching arms he threw gems, rubies, sapphires, emeralds and gold among the crowd that had gathered round the tower from all the four quarters of the world. What was the meaning of this strange dream? King Suddhodana tried to find an interpreter for the dreams which seemed to him a forecast of coming woe.

At last an old hermit came and said: "Grieve not, Great King, for all seven dreams show that your son, though he will leave the world, will spread the jewels of his teachings over all lands and peace and contentment will reign. Try not to hinder him, for he must go."

But the old King, in his fear of losing his son, ordered double watchers at the gates of Prince Siddhartha's pleasure gardens, and commanded that all the movements of the prince should be carefully watched.

Prince Siddhartha was now always deep in thought, and the desire grew in him to see the real life with its sorrows and joys, its light and shade, beyond his own small realm. He wanted to see the city without decorations, the worker in his work-a-day clothes and when all people were not aware of his coming.

He asked the king to let him go afoot among the people without his princely ornaments. The old King reluctantly consented. And so, one day, Channa and a few other faithful servants accompanied Prince Siddhartha into the city, to have a look at the side of lowly life. He was interested in all he saw and life seemed good to him, this life of toil and yet content, compared with that of learning and of teaching. He almost began to believe that those who were not princes might be even happier than the high-born.

But there, near the Southern gate, he met a sight which turned his heart sick. A poor man, seemin gly stricken with a dreadful disease, was lying groaning on the ground. The sick man gasped for breath and moaned,

"Oh, take me to my hut, good people, that I may die there."

Prince Siddhartha started, and kneeling down, laid the poor man's head on his knees. "O Channa," he cried, "what a dreadful sight! Can such illness come to any man who lives?"

"Yes," answered Channa, "and even to you, My Prince, if you nurse this man, who seems to be stricken with plague. Let us take him to his own place."

"So all people live in fear of illness." thought the prince, "and then comes death! How then can life be sweet for me and mine? Let me turn home to think and find out what can be done."

And thus he turned to go back to the palace. But at the Western gate another sight met his eyes, which made him shudder. On a bier, carried by some wailing men, lay stiff and straight a corpse ready for the funeral pyre. Flowers were strewn over him but the surrounding mourners moaned and wept.

"There comes the dead," said Channa. "Prince, thus death comes to us all; it comes to young and old, to rich and poor."

"O world!" cried Siddhartha, "I see now thy want! I see what need there is of comfort to all mankind! Even to the happy ones come sickness and death. The veil that clouded my eyes is rent. I shall go to find out how I can help." And he turned his steps homeward.

But another sight met his eyes near the Northern gate. It was a Monk who walked with bright eyes and steady steps on the road. He had no possessions but his begging bowl and his seven-knotted stick. His head and feet were bare, but yet he looked contented. "I seek the way to deliverance" he answered when asked whither he went.

"And so will I," softly said Prince Siddhartha and he entered into his prison-pleasure-house to think and meditate, and then—to leave.

Here in the palace all was peace and joy and happiness. They all had fallen asleep during their games and songs, the sweet companicns of the princess. Yasodhara also slept.

When the prince entered, he lay down beside her. Then, while thinking of the coming pain of parting from her, he heard her move and moan , and questioned her. She said : "I dreamed that a snow-white bull came running through the town. A jewel was on his forehead, which shone with great splendour. The bull ran up to me and I put my arms round his neck and asked him to stay. But he broke from my arms and disappeared."

"Then I saw the flag, which was flying in honour of Indra, fall down from the temple and another flag hoisted, covered with jewels and with curious writing. The wind came and unfurled it and many people arrived and read the writing. All were glad on understanding its meaning. And wonderful flowers, other than our flowers, covered the ground before the flag. This was all good, but then a voice called out 'The time has come.'"

"I seemed to wake up then," Yasodhara continued, "and I searched for Thee, my Lord, at my side; but I found thee not, only an empty robe was there instead of thee. What does this mean? Then my jewelled belt fell off, my bangles dropped, the flowers in my hair withered and the royal parasol above my head was broken.

"I looked round wildly and then I heard the far-away lowing of the white bull. What does this mean, my Lord? My heart is full of fear. Thou canst not leave me and thy child and all those who love thee. Speak a word of comfort to thy loving wife!"

Siddhartha bent down to his wife and spoke gently: "To comfort thee, my faithful wife, hear what I say. My love to thee is changeless, and even if thy dreams may be shadows of things to come to thee and to me, be sure my love is with thee always. Thou knowest I have mused and thought how I could help the world. When the time comes I must go, for I love thee. What I do is for thee, because in thee I love all creatures. Be comforted and sleep. Let me watch and think!"

This was the farewell to his loving Yasodhara. He saw her love would be a tie so firm that it would hold him if he waited any longer. So, while she slept in tears, he saw the moon look into the window. It was full moon and the moon was in the Zodiacal sign of the Crab, and it seemed as if the Devas whispered:

"Take thy choice, this is the night of thy departure. The world groans under its weight of woe. Come and save the world! Thy time has come."

He longed to kiss his sleeping wife farewell. He yearned to take his baby son into his arms for the last time. But no! he dared not do it. For if they waked up and wept, how could he leave them?

Prince Siddhartha bowed down reverently at Yasodhara's feet and he walked round her thrice. She had been true to him and loving in many lives, and with bitter tears of parting in his dimmed eyes, he looked and looked and then softly he let fall the curtain which divided Yasodhara's room from the hall where her friends and companions slept.

Away he walked with faltering steps, away from love and beauty and pleasure. But the time had come and he was ready, although his heart was almost broken.

"Awake, Channa, my faithful friend," he cried. "Saddle me my snow white horse, my Kanthaka, for the last time, for I must go."

"Go whither?" asked Channa. "Go whither in the night, away from wife, child, father, and kingdom?"

"Hold me not back, my friend," answered the Prince, sweetly. "The time has come and I must go."

Sighing heavily, Channa went to bring Kanthaka, who in his marble stable, looked at Channa with waking eyes.

"But how to get through all these locked gates?" thought Channa. "How to pass the watching crowds of warriors?" Do not wonder, thou faithful servant of the Lord! The time has come, thy Lord will be allowed to pass! And lo! the gates were opened by invisible hands of Devas. The watchers slept a deep unconscious sleep and Prince Siddhartha rode through the gates on Kanthaka's back, only followed by Channa. No sound was heard, for even Kanthaka's hoofs, which always made a proud loud noise on the pavement when he bore Prince Siddhartha, were hushed. No one heard the Prince fleeing from wife and child, from home and kingdom to become a pilgrim, a wanderer, till he should find how he could help the world.

The world slept when the great Renunciation was fulfilled. But the bright moon saw it and the stars twinkled their approval.

CHAPTER VI.

THE LAST RIDE ON KANTHAKA.

On Kanthaka rushed to bear the prince away. Siddhartha's head drooped, for his heart was filled with woe. Separation weighed heavily upon him. But he must go on now, as the misery of the world was greater than

Kantaka waiting to be saddled

the grief of wife and child, of father and friends.

So he rode on through the night until the morning star glittered and the new sun's first ray shone on the water of the river Anoma, the bordering stream of King Suddhodana's kingdom.

Here Siddhartha got down from Kanthaka's back, caressed him gently and thus spoke to Channa, the faithful : "Thou hast followed me to the end of King Suddhodana's kingdom. I shall never forget that. It will ever bring thee joy. Take now my Kanthaka back and also my princely jewels and my royal robe. I need them not. With them take also my long hair, it cannot be my ornament any more."

With these words, Siddhartha cut off his long, waving hair with his sword, and he handed every thing to Channa and asked him to tell his father, the King, not to grieve ; for he would come back to him, when he had become more than prince or king, when full of wisdom : for all realms on earth would be his own. "For," cried he, "I have cast away *my* world to save the whole world."

Then Siddhartha turned away and wandered into the forest, now no more a prince but a lonely wanderer, a pilgrim, seeking the salvation of the world.

And the weeping Channa turned back leading Kanthaka, who carried now only the jewels, sword and locks of his dear master.

There was wailing and lamenting in the palace when the messenger returned. But they all understood that this had to come; for the prophecy had said that either he would become a great ruler on earth or the greatest ruler of the heaven-world. Now the choice was made, how dare they complain? He left only to save them all.

And Yasodhara throw off her jewels and her royal sari and said: "I am a widow, give me my widow's gown and let me humbly pray for his return as the Great One who will save me as he will save the world!

She knew that it was love for her and for all, that made him leave. She knew and she understood, for he had told her that he loved her well. She would not keep him from his great work. In her mind's eye she saw him already as the Saviour of the world and with uplifted hands she cried, "I was Thine often and I am Thine now. When Thou hast reached Thy high aim, I shall be Thy humble follower."

Thus sweet Yasodhara retired and lived the life of a widow, and she brought up her son Rāhula in awe and love for the father who had left a Prince, but who would come back a Saint.

VII.

THE PILGRIM.

Siddhartha, who was now a humble pilgrim with monkish robes and wooden alms-bowl, went on, along the highroad. One day he came to King Bimbisāra's kingdom. He entered the capital and stood with bowed head before the door of some humble workman's house, as was the custom, begging for food. The people who saw him wondered who this holy man could be, for shining was his face, and noble was his look. His whole appearance showed that he was of high birth, for he walked erect as if accustomed to bear a crown and not a shaven head. His alms bowl was filled quickly, for every woman who saw him eagerly ran in to her hut and came out with a cake or some fruit or whatever her humble household could spare. The mother held up her small child to him to bless it, or she asked the older ones to kiss the hem of the robe of this Shramana who looked so holy.

Thus with his bowl filled to overflowing, the Bodhisattva went to the jungle to eat the food so lovingly given to him, before the sun reached the meridian.

King Bimbisāra found the Bodhisattva sitting quietly under a shady tree. The king had heard from his attendants, that a holy monk had entered his capital, and, being a pious. man, he came himself to get advice from him who was shining with holiness, as he was told.

"Who art thou," the king asked, "who comest to bring gladness to the hearts of my subjects? Thy looks betray thy noble birth. If thou hast no home, come and share my kingdom with me!"

Sweetly smiling, the Bodhisattva answered: "If I wanted to rule, I could have done so, for I possessed a kingdom and great riches. But I am searching for those riches which are not of this world. I search for *truth*, my King, and how I can deliver humanity from misery, from fear of sickness and from death. So, go in peace and let me wander on!"

"Then, after thou hast found what thou dost seek, Oh, let me know and let me become thy disciple," pleaded the king.

"Be it so," said the Bodhisattva, and on he went to seek the teachers Ālāra and Udraka, who lived in the forest, and who were said to be wise teachers of the law. He sat at their feet and he listened to their teachings and he mused and meditated, but no satisfaction came to his mind.

Then he saw the priests in the temples sacrificing animals to the Gods, and sadness filled his heart. "It can only be ignorance," he thought, "which makes them try to appease the wrath of the Gods by shedding blood! Can blood purify and wipe out sins? Oh no! that is not right and not the way to destroy the evil. To give up hatred and to love all creatures, that must be the right sacrifice and the true worship."

The Bodhisattva could not stay here and so he went in search of different teachings. And he came to the jungle of Uruvela and he found there five Ascetics, who practised austere self-discipline. He admired their earnestness and he joined them.

While they were severe in striving to subdue the desires of their bodies, while they hurt their bodies and starved them, he tortured and starved his body more than they. At last they acknowledged him as their Master and they revered him as such.

For six years the Bodhisattva remained in the jungle of Uruvela and his body was like a skeleton, for he swallowod every day only one grain of rice or hemp seed. He hoped thus to cross the bridge from life to death and to find deliverance.

But he had not found true wisdom which he had hoped to find, and he was not satisfied. When musing under a jambu-tree he thought: "This cannot be the right path, for my body is so weak that my mind cannot think. My fasting has not advanced me in the path of salvation. I must strengthen my body by food and drink and seek on further." He got up from his seat under the jambu-tree and took a bath in the river near, but he was so weak that he could hardly get out of the water. He staggered and fell and a deep unconsciousness came over him. His five companions thought he was dead and they worshipped him as a saint. But he recovered and sank down under a tree, where Sujata the daughter of a herdsman found him. She offered him milk-rice[23] which she had specially prepared to offer to some holy man. When the Bodhisattva had taken some milk-rice, new life came back to his body. But his five companions turned away from him and said : "He is going back to earth life, he is not a saint."

The Bodhisattva resolved that he would leave them and wander on to find full understanding and enlightenment.

So the Bodhisattva started on a new pilgrimage. On his way, he heard the pattering of many feet and when he looked round he saw some herdsmen driving a flock of sheep on the high-road. It was noon-time and the fierce sun-rays scorched the poor animals. The Bodhisattva asked the herdsmen why they drove the poor sheep just in the heat of the sun. "Oh," answered the herdsmen, "we have to hurry, for our king is making a great sacrifice tonight and we must be there in time for it with these sheep."

"Then I will go also," said the Bodhisattva, and, picking up in his arms a poor limping lamb, that could not follow the herd, he walked along with the herdsmen.

While he was walking on, with the sick lamb in his arms, a poor distracted mother stood before him and cried with uplifted hands and tear bedimmed eyes. "Lord, Thou hadst pity on me yesterday and badest me cure my child by mustard seeds, begged from a house where neither son nor daughter nor friend had ever died. I cannot find such a house or hut, for there has been death everywhere. Now my poor babe is dead. Is there no help?"

"My sister," said the Bodhisattva gently "thou hast found what every body has to find and that is, that not thou alond hast to suffer. See, thy child was already dead when thou askedst me to cure it yesterday. Thy heart was so much stricken with woe, that I had to show thee, in order to cure thee, that every human being has to suffer the same woe as thou, for there was no cure for thy dead child. I myself search for the secret to cure the woe which death brings. Cremate thy child, my sister, and think that life is suffering and death comes to all."

With these gentle words the Bodhisattva turned and followed the herd of sheep and with them entered the capital where the sacrifice was to be performed. The people on the road stared at the holy man bearing the lamb in his arms and wondered at his beaming face. They saw him going into the temple with the sacrificial sheep and they followed him to find out what he had to do with the sacrifice which the king wanted to perform.

All entered the temple and there the king stood, at his side the priests in white robes, with sharp knives in their hands, ready for the slaying of the animals which were laid on the bloody altars beside the flickering sacrificial flames.

Quietly the Bodhisattva stepped forward. Raising his right hand and pointing to the priest he cried out: "Oh king, let him not strike." And he stepped to the altar and loosened the bands of the goat which was to be sacrificed that moment.

Nobody stopped the Bodhisattva's hand, for all were overawed. And he lifted his voice and with his glorious eyes moved with pity and compassion he spoke: "Kill not, Oh King, for thou hast not the power to give life! No blood of these poor beasts, which love life as we do, can atone for thy sins. How can the blood of unwilling victims reconcile merciless Gods? If man is merciless towards these victims, which pray for mercy, how canst thou think that the Gods will have pity on thee and forgive thy sins? These animals have trust in thee, they give thee milk and wool and look upon thee as a God! Therefore have mercy on them as thou askest for mercy from the Gods."

The King wondered and drew near, stopping the priest in his ghastly work with hands uplifted. The priests, abashed, covered their blood-stained knives and hands with their cloaks.

"Life would be so fair," the Bodhisattva continued, "if there reigned love and pity and mercy. The Gods themselves then would be the Gods of Mercy and not the Gods of Wrath."

So convincingly and so gently did the Bodhisattva preach, that the priests extinguished the sacrificial fires, and then the

King had proclaimed through his realm, that no bloody sacrifice should be given to the Gods. He also had proclaimed that it was his will that no animals should be killed for food in his whole kingdom. Grains and vegetables and fruits should be the food for his subjects from that great day forward.

The king who made this proclamation was King Bimbisāra. When he had recognised the Bodhisattva, he begged him to stay with him and teach him and his subjects.

"Not yet, my King" the Bodhisattva answered, "I have not yet found the goal. I cannot remain. Worldly pleasures do not tempt me. Let me follow my road. I will walk to Gaya and there, under the forest trees, I hope to find what I have searched for in many lives. For know, Oh King, not by fasting and torturing the body, not by studying the Shastras, Vedas and Purānas, can we find the perfect light. It comes to us from the Great Light which illumines the Inner Being and that is what I long to find. I walked the Path for countless lives, and now I shall become the Path myself. Farewell, My King. When you see me next, I shall be dead, but I shall live as the Buddha."

Thus speaking, the Bodhisattva walked away, his body shining like a sparkling star, his eyes filled with heavenly light.

VIII.

UNDER THE BODHI TREE

The Bodhisattva walked on. He walked on flowers, but he saw them not. The Devas strewed them on his path. The branches of the trees under which he walked bent down to shade him. The birds sang their sweetest songs for him. So he reached Gaya,[24] where he intended to sit down and meditate till he had found what he had searched for so long.

"Give me a handful of your Kusa grass," the Bodhisattva called out to the grass-cutter Swastika, who was occupied in spreading out of the mown grass, which lay around in sweet-smelling heaps.

"Certainly I will, my Lord," the humble grass-cutter answered. "Here is grass, as much as Thou wouldst have. And may it be a soft couch to Thee, Oh Holy one, whose shining face shows heavenly bliss." Thrice Swastika bowed down and then he went away and the Bodhisattva was alone.

Holy stillness filled the air; all nature seemed expectant and hushed silence was everywhere. The small voices of nature even seemed subdued in awe, for the Lord had sunk into deep meditation.

Only Māra was in great anxiety. That Evil One had in a dream seen that his stronghold had been shattered and that all his evil

Mara's Attack.

attempts on mankind were destroyed. "On, my armies of evil!" he cried in despair. "Search for the Great One under the Bodhi-tree. Take all your arrows of hate, passion and lust with you, take all the evil maids who tempt the weak, take all the rocks of temptation which you can find and destroy the One who is now at the point of gaining enlightenment."

So the whole army of the Evil One came rushing on, Māra at its head. They assaulted with all their force the Holy One who sat under the Bo-tree in deep meditation. They aimed all the arrows of hate, fear, temptation on him, but they failed. Then rocks came flying at him, those rocks of ambition, riches and others that they could find, which they thought must conquer him. But all was in vain. All stones thrown at him, changed into flowers: all flames spit at him from the mouths of Demons, turned into divine light.

Then Māra called his fairest daughters and one of them took the shape of Yasodhara, and with pleading face, and eyes bedimmed with tears, she stood before him. "Come back to me, my Lord my King," she sighed, "I die with longing for Thee."

"Thou art not real," called out the Bodhisattva. "Go to thy evil home, I know the one whom thou wouldst represent. She is not here. Be gone all, ye cannot blind my seeing eyes."

And lo! a great weeping sound of dismay filled the air. Māra was conquered with all his armies of evil, and they fled in terror and confusion.

All was still again. It was the first watch of the night, then a veil was withdrawn from his inner sight and the Bodhisattva came to the knowledge of all his former births. He saw himself as bird, animal, human being. He saw how he had striven to get better and higher every new birth, and how in giving away his limbs, his eyes, his wife and children, his body through his compassion and truthfulness, he had gained the right to come to this high stage of perfection.

In the middle watch of the night another veil left his inner sight, and he saw and recognized all conditions of present life on earth[25] and of the future, all systems of the worlds, all rulers of the Universe. All light and shadow of life was spread before his divine sight.

And at the time when the beating of the drum announces the breaking of the day, the last watch of the night, when people sleep the soundest, then the knowledge, which points out the Path to Nirvana, the secret of the Sorrow of the World, the Four Noble Truths, burst upon him. All veils that had clouded his vision were gone. The long search was finished, He had become the Buddha, the All-Knowing, the All-Wise, the Tathāgata.

Why was the world so glad on that bright morning? Why did all nature smile? All birds were singing and all animals were in peace. All flowers sent out their sweetest odour.

"Know ye all who mourn and grieve, the Buddha has been born, the world is saved. Rejoice all ye who can hear and see!" The Devas hailed the morning star "It is finished." The birds sang, "It is finished." *

The Lord Buddha, the Blessed One, rising from his seat of kusa-grass under the Bodhi-tree, stretched out his arms over the world and spoke:

Many a House of Life
Hath held me—Seeking ever Him, who wrought
These prisons of the senses, sorrow-fraught;
Sore was my ceaseless strife!
But now,
Thou Builder of this Tabernacle—Thou!
I know Thee! Never shalt Thou build again
These walls of pain,
Nor raise the Roof-tree of deceits, nor lay
Fresh rafters on the clay;
Broken Thy house is, and the ridge-pole split!
Delusion fashioned it!
Safe pass I thence—Deliverance to obtain [26]

Seven more weeks did Lord Buddha muse and meditate and think and never food passed his lips. But then all was clear and he rose to teach the world, his face shown like the sun, his body like the moon-beams. Yes! those who saw with more than human eyes, saw the rays of Buddha-hood round him, which shone as glorious colours and which drew to him those who had been born to become his disciples and his followers.

---

* This occurred on a Fullmoon-Day of Wesak.

IX.

LORD BUDDHA'S FIRST SERMOM

After seven times seven days had passed, there came two merchants near the Bodhi-tree. When they saw the Buddha they wondered at his shining body and his glorious face. "Let us offer some food to this Holy One," they said. And humbly bowing down to him, they offered him some rice cakes and honey. He silently accepted and he ate. This was the first food the Buddha tasted after He had reached Buddhahood. He blessed the two merchants and spoke words of wisdom to them.

Tapussa and Bhallika were the names of these two merchants. They kept the words of the Buddha in their hearts and they said: "We take our Refuge in Thee Lord and in Thy Teaching. Let us become Thy pupils." And as He consented, these two merchants became the first lay disciples of the Lord Buddha.

But when the merchants had gone, doubt came to the Buddha whether mankind would understand the difficult Dharma which He had to preach. 'How can I make them understand?" he mused. Then Brahmā Sahampati, fearing that the Buddha would not teach, came down from Brahma-Loka, bowed down before the Tathāgata and said: "If the Holy One does not teach, the world must perish! Have Thou compassion on it, Oh Lord! Thou knowest that there are some whose understanding is only clouded by a thin veil. Thou knowest also that there are pure souls, who are yet helplessly entangled in the snares of sorrow."

And the Lord said: "Wide open be the door of Immortality to all who have ears to hear. May they receive the Dharma with faith.* I will go and teach. But who shall be the first ones to hear? I will find my five companions and former disciples, who live now in the Deer-Park near Benares and I will preach to them; for they are yet torturing their bodies and think that they can thus attain Salvation."

And the Tathāgata started on his way to the Deer-Park. While on the road, Upaka, a young Jain, a former friend of Prince Siddhartha, saw the Buddha and marvelled at his beauty and asked Him: "What makes Thy face shine so serenely? Hast Thou found the goal Thou searchest for?" "I have found Nirvana," answered the Buddha, "and I am now on my way to found the Kingdom of Righteousness and Truth on Earth."

Upaka did not understand. He shook his head and went another way.

The Buddha walked on and when He came to the Deer Park, He saw the five ascetics

* Paul Carus, Gospel of Buddha.

sitting on their seats of Kusa-grass, but they did not move when He approached. They had agreed among themselves that they would not greet Him, because they thought He had left the ascetic life and had become again a lover of the world.

When the Buddha stood before them, they were so struck with His holy appearance, that as with one accord they jumped up from their seats. But still they called him Gautama and 'friend' and asked Him where He came from.

"Do not call me 'friend'" He answered, "for I am the Buddha, the Holy One. Call me Father, for I look upon all as my children."

Then the Buddha began to explain to the five Ascetics, that they could not attain Salvation by torturing their bodies, for the mind cannot think when the body is starved and in pain. He taught them the Middle-Path, which He had found, and He said, "He who fills his lamp with water instead of oil cannot light up the darkness."

When they were willing to hear more, the Buddha preached to them that beautiful *First Sermon*, which (the old books say) the Saints from Heaven and the Devas from their abode and even the animals from the forest came to hear. All listened with rapt attention, and all understood it (it is said) in their own language.

The Buddha taught them the four Noble Truths[27]: he taught them the Noble Eightfold Path[28] which, in a nutshell, comprises all the Buddhist teachings.

Thus in the Deer-Park at Benares the Buddha set the Wheel of the Law rolling, in which the 'spokes are the rules of pure conduct; justice is the uniformity of their length; wisdom is the tire; modesty and thoughtfulness are the hub in which the immovable axle of Truth is fixed.'

And the ice of ill-will had melted from the hearts of the five ascetics, and they and all who listened called out: "Hail to the Buddha, the Tathāgata, Who has found the Truth and the whole Law of Righteousness and Truth. Good-will and Peace will reign for ever among men."

And the oldest of the five Ascetics spoke first to the Buddha. His name was Kondañño. He said: "Truly I take my Refuge in the Lord. May I be allowed to become Thy disciple?" The Buddha replied: "If ye have understood my teachings, sons, stand together, for if ye stand alone, ye are not strong: stand together and preach the Truth. I bind you together as my first disciples. Through you five, I found the Sangha (Priesthood) who must teach the Dharma (the Law) to the world."

And the five disciples uttered solemnly the three Refuges[29] [30]: "I take my Refuge in the Buddha, I take my Refuge in the Dharma, I take my Refuge in the Sangha."

X.

NEW DISCIPLES

When Yashas, a rich merchant's son in Benares, heard of the Buddha, he came and implored the Tathāgata to teach him. He invited Him also to come to his father's house. The Buddha consented, and there, not only Yashas, but also his wife, his father and mother, became His lay disciples.

The more the Buddha preached, the more the people gathered round Him and many became disciples and began to lead a holy life. There were so many that the Lord Buddha saw he could not teach them all. So he said to his Monks: "Bhikkhus [31] ! Go out and preach the Doctrine which I have taught you. Preach the Doctrine which is glorious in the beginning, glorious in the middle and glorious in the end."

From this time, it was during the month of October (wap) that Lord Buddha sent out His Disciples to preach the Law, it became the custom that the Bhikkhus wandered out in fair weather, as their Master did, and in the rainy season they gathered round the Tathāgata and received new instructions.

In his wanderings the Buddha also came to Uruvela, where the Jatilas lived, who worshipped Fire. Kashyapa was their leader. He had heard about the Tathāgata and he was curious to see him. When he entered the city, the Buddha went to Kashyapa and asked his permission to spend the night in the room where the Sacred Fire was kept. Kashyapa answered: "I would let Thee remain there, for Thou art holy, but there is a serpent in the room, which might kill Thee."

The Buddha smiled and still insisted on his staying in the room. In the night the serpent came, but it could not harm the Holy One and in anger it died. Also the Holy Fire went out. When Kashyapa saw in the morning what had happened, he threw all the implements of the Fire-Worship into the river and he and all his followers became disciples of the Lord Buddha.

Then the Buddha, accompanied by Kashyapa and the Jatilas went to Maghada, where King Bimbisāra lived. Bimbisāra, when he heard of his coming, met Him with all his household. The Buddha preached a wonderful sermon in Maghada.

He also accepted King Bimbisāra's invitation to the palace for a meal with His Bhikkhus. The King was very happy and said: "I had five desires in this life and all the five are now fulfilled. The fifth and greatest was to have heard Thee and to understand Thee. Take me as Thy disciple. I take my Refuge in the Buddha, the Dharma and the Sangha."

The Buddha blessed him and accepted him.

Then Bimsāra spoke: "My Lord, my pleasure-garden Vānuvana is not too near the city and not too far. It is shady and it is cool ; it is healthy and just suited for retired life. Accept it for Thyself and Thy fraternity, as a dwelling place."

The Buddha silently gave his consent and thus He and His Bhikkhus often dwelt there in the monsoon times and He taught there.

At this time, it was on a Full-moon day of Navan-month (February) that Sariputra and Moggalana, who afterwards became very renowned, began to be his disciples. Where-ever the Buddha went people followed Him and listened to His teachings.

Anāthapindika, a very charitable and rich man, called the Father of Orphans, met the Buddha at Rajāgriha and requested Him to come to Shrāvasti, the capital of Kola, where he lived and where he wished to build a Temple and dedicate it to the fraternity. The Buddha promised to go there later on and he sent Sariputra with Anāthapindika to select the place, while he himself prepared to visit his father, who had sent word to him : "I wish to see my son before I die. Others have had the benefit of Thy teaching, but not Thy father and Thy relatives." And so he walked, accompanied by many Bhikkhus and other people to Kapilavastu, his father's city.

When the old king Suddhodana heard that his son was approaching the city, he got into his royal chariot to meet him. But when he came near Him and saw his son on foot, accompanied by many disciples, he had the chariot stopped and got out. He started at the sight of the noble figure of the Buddha dressed in a mean yellow garment and yet looking more than a prince. How he yearned to clasp Him in his arms and call out: "My son, my son, come back to me." But he dared not speak and his lips closed in mingled grief and joy.

At last he said, seating himself before his son: "It is now seven years since I saw Thee last. How my heart has longed for Thee!"

And the Buddha saw the old king's heart almost breaking and he said: "I know, my King, that thy heart is full of love for thy son. But give that love to all thy subjects and then thou canst receive thy son as the Buddha, the teacher of Truth. Then will the peace of Nirvāna enter thy heart."

The old king clasped his bands in happiness and yet in agony and said: "A great change has come for me and I accept Thy teachings. Teach the world and also me. I see the fruit of Thy Renuciation."

The old, King went back to his palace and the Buddha remained in a grove near the city.

XI.

YASODHARA

The following morning the Buddha took his earthen almsbowl and begged for food. The women gave him what food they had with joyful hearts and solemn eyes. But when this news came to the old king, "Sire, thy son begs for his food in his own country, where he ought to rule," then the old king became angry, got on his horse and, seeing his son standing with bent head and his begging bowl in his hand before a lowly hut, and a woman bowing low before him, he stopped and asked: "Why, my son, how canst Thou beg here in Thine own land, where Thou shouldst give alms instead of asking for it?"

"That is the rule of my race," answered the Holy One gently. "Thy race, my son, is the race of Kings; they do not beg!" I speak of the race of Buddhas," the Holy One answered. "They beg for their food." "Come to the palace, son," the king pleaded, "Bring Thy disciples with Thee and honour me by accepting food for all."

The Buddha consented.

Just an hour before noon-tide a procession of yellow-robed monks entered the palace of King Suddhodana and there they were royally fed; but each using his begging bowl only for the food.

King Suddhodana pleaded over and over again, that his son should take back his kingdom and rule in righteousness and teach in wisdom. But gently and firmly the Buddha replied: "My King, thy realm is not vast enough for me. My Kingdom is the heaven-world. Do not urge me any more, for I could not let the world become an orphan and be the father of this, thy kingdom only."

The old King became silent, big tears rolling down his withered cheeks. Then he said "Then take me as Thy pupil, for the last days of my present life must be spent in Thy presence and with Thy blessing."

" Be it so, as thou wishest, my King."

The Buddha looked around and saw all his relatives and friends, but the one who had been his wife, when he was Prince Siddhartha, was not there. "Where is Yasodhara?" he asked. The old King answered: "My son, her grief was great, her mourning for Thee cannot be described. She cut her hair, she discarded her royal robes. She lived a widow's life all these seven years. She would not come to great Thee, fearing that the woe and yet the happiness of seeing Thee again would be too much for her. Wilt Thou go and see her?"

"Yes, I will," the Buddha said, "for she has earned this favour by her faithfulness not only in this life, but it many lives."

The Buddha went to Yasodhara and said to the two disciples who accompanied him: "Do not disturb her, if she touches me. I am free, but she is yet bound with ties which I will sever now."

He entered her chamber, where she sat in widow's garb, with tearful, longing eyes. She was quite overcome when she saw the beautiful holy face and yellow robe of him whom she had mourned for seven long years.

With one long wail of agony she fell at His feet and clasping her thin arms round His holy feet she burst out into tears. When the first outburst of grief and joy was over He said gently: "Sit down, Yasodhara, and listen. Dost thou not know that once, when we were happily together, thou hadst the great desire to become the wife of the future Buddha? Now see, that has come to thee now. Thy Karma is fulfilled and unspeakable joy will follow, as thou hast fulfilled thy mission."

"Take me as Thy pupil" she humbly said, "my grief is over and heavenly joy fills now my once lonely heart."

And the Buddha taught His father and Yasodhara and they became His disciples. She was the first woman disciple together with Prajāpati, His former foster-mother

---

XII.

RAHULA

When the people in Kapilavastu heard that their King was following the teachings of his son, who had become the Tathāgata, many of them did likewise and also Ananda, the half-brother of the Buddha, and Devadatta his cousin, joined him. Anurudha, the philosopher and Upāli, the barber, became His disciples at this time.

Yosodhara, now quite happy, said, after seven days had passed, to her son Rāhula: "Go, my son, and ask thy father, the Holy Muni with the beautiful face, for thy inheritance! He has four great mines of wealth, tell him that thou, as his son and heir, ought to have them as thine inheritance."

Rāhula went, as he was told and looking wistfully into the face of the Buddha he whispered: "My father." The Buddha turned his face to him and Rāhula said:" My mother bids me ask for my inheritance."

"I have neither gold nor silver, my son, but if thou wishest to receive such treasures that are not of this world, I am willing to give thee the four Truths and the Eight-fold Noble Path. But art thou strong enough to live these Truths, for thou art young in years?"

"I am strong," Rāhula answered, "I want to follow Thee."

And so Rāhula was also accepted into the Brotherhood and King Suddhodana had lost all those of his relatives who could have become his successors on his throne. But still the old King followed the Buddha, and his Kingdom after his death, came into the hands of others.

XIII.

THE JETAVANA

In the meanwhile Anāthapindika, the father of the orphans, had reached his father's town with Sāriputra, whom the Buddha had sent with him.

There they searched for a garden suitable for the Buddhist Fraternity. They found a garden, which belonged to Jeta, the son of the King of Shrāvasti. They wished to purchase it, but the prince only consented to sell it if Anāthapindika would cover the area of the garden with gold pieces. Anāthapindika commenced to spread out his gold, when the prince heard why he was so anxious to give his enormous wealth for the garden.

" If that is the purpose of your purchase, my friend," the prince said " I do not want your wealth. Let us share the gift. you shall only purchase the land and I will give the trees."

Both together built a lofty Vihāra and pouring the water of donation over Sāriputra's hands, they dedicated the Vihāra, the forest and the whole land to the Buddhist Brotherhood throughout the whole world.

The Buddha was asked to come and take possession of it and so He left Kapilavastu with his disciples, and from that time he spent most of the rainy seasons with his numerous followers at the Jetavana.

The King of the land, Prasēnajit also listened to the words of the Buddha; he kept them in his heart and became a wise and worthy King.

XIV.

THE BUDDHA ATTAINS PARI-NIRVANA

Wandering about from land to land the Tathāgata taught and preached for forty-five years.

Then, when his Mission was fulfilled, and his Doctrine could be preached by his faithful Bhikkhus, he was ready to leave his physical body.

He walked with many of his disciples to the Sāla-Grove[32] of the Mallas, the Upavartana of Kusinagara, near the Himālayas. And there he had his couch spread, as he knew that his earthly wanderings would soon be over.

He called his disciples to his side and specially Ananda, his faithful companion, who had never left him since he became his disciple. Ananda was overcome with grief, when he saw that the Buddha was ready to leave his physical body, and he had hidden himself to weep alone. When he was called the Buddha saw his grief and said "Do not be troubled. It is the nature of earthly things that they must perish. Truth alone will ever remain! I have fulfilled my Mission. You, my Ananda, have done well. Be earnest in your efforts and soon you too shall be free."

"In due time another Buddha will come to teach the world the same eternal Truths which I have taught you. His disciples will number many thousands as mine now count many hundreds. His name will be Maitriya (Compassion)."

Then the Mallas came and asked to see the Buddha. He admitted them and preached to them and then an old mendicant, Subhadra, pleaded to see the Lord. He also was taught by the Buddha, and he became His last disciple.

And the Lord Buddha asked: "Is there anyone, who has any doubt about the Buddha, or about the Truth of the Dharma?" No one answered, and Ananda said: "There is none here who doubts." "Have you all understood, and seen and felt and realized the Truth?" the Lord asked. "We have, Lord," Ananda whispered.

Once more the Buddha spoke. "I exhort you, decay is inherent in all component things, but the Truth will remain for ever. Apply yourselves with diligence."

Then the Lord Buddha passed from deep meditation, through the four dhyânas[33] into Pari-Nirvâna.[34]

And a mighty earthquake shook the earth. The lightnings flashed and the thunder rolled.

The disciples of the Lord Buddha cried out: "Too soon has the Blessed-One left us! Too soon has the Light of the world gone out."

But the venerable Anuradha exhorted the brethren and said, "enough, my brethren. Weep not, neither lament! Has not the Lord declared, that we must separate from those near and dear to us? Those who are free from passion will bear the loss calm and self-possessed, mindful of the truth He has taught us." Both the reverend Anuradha and Ananda spent the rest of the night in religious discourse!

It was on a Full-moon Day of Wesak (May) that the Blessed-One left this earth !full-moon day.

Then the Mallas of Kusinagara gathered together perfumes and garlands and went to the Sola-Grove where the body of the Blessed One lay. And they treated the remains of the body of the Blessed-One as they would have done, if he had been an earthly King. When the funeral-pyre was lit (it is said) the sun and moon withdrew their shining, the earth shook, while flowers showered down like rain from heaven.

When the cremation was over Dêvaputra said to the multitude assembled: "The earthly remains of the Blessed One have been cremated, but the Truth He taught will live for ever! Let us go out into the world and preach to all the "Four Noble Truths" and the "Noble Eight-fold Path."

And ambassadors from all parts of India came and took the relics of the body of the Buddhā from the funeral-ground and they divided them into eight parts and the Kings had dagabas erected over them.

Some of these relics have lately been unearthed and they are revered by numberless Buddhists.

Worship the High-One, the Exalted One,
Worship Him in *Service* !
Worship Him with great Awe !
For the Great-One the Exalted One·
Had fullfilled His Mission.
His last birth on Earth was finished
On a Fullmoon-Day of Wesak.

NOTES

1. Page ix. WESAK-DAY. This is the Full-moon Day in the month of Wesak (May). Buddhists celebrate Wesak-Day not only as the birthday of the Lord Buddha (born 623 years before Christ), but also; he became Buddha on the Full-moon Day of Wesak and he entered Parinirvāna on the Full-moon Day of that month. It is said also that he paid his third visit to Lanka on a full-moon day of Wesak. So there is a fourfold celebration on Wesak-Day. This particular Wesak-Day mentioned in the Introduction was in the year 1913.

2. Page ix. ATTHA-SILA OR ATTHĀNGA SĪLA.—The eightfold Precepts as distinguished from the Pancha Sila, or fivefold Precepts, which are generally recited in Pali every morning and evening in good Buddhist houses, are taken by Buddhists at special religious festivities. The people then put on white clothes and they do not eat any food after midday till the next morning. They spend their time in meditation and contemplation and listen to Bana preaching (Sermons) all night long.

The Five Precepts are:—

(i) I observe the precept to abstain from destroying the life of beings.

(ii) I observe the precept to abstain from stealing.

(iii) I observe the precept to abstain from unlawful sexual intercourse.

(iv) I observe the precept to abstain from falsehood.

(v) I observe the precept to abstain from using drugs and intoxicants.

(The three following precepts are added when Attha-Sīla is taken.)

(vi) I observe the precept to abstain from eating at an unseasonable time (after midday.)

(vii) I observe the precept to abstain from dancing, singing, shows, theatres and amusements.

(viii) I observe the precept to abstain from using high and broad beds.

3. Page ix. MAHINDA was the son of the Indian Buddhist Emperor Dharmasoka, who lived about 300 B.C. Mahinda and his sister Sangamitta were the first Buddhist Missionaries who came to Ceylon, and who devoted their lives to the spread of Buddhism in Ceylon. They came during the reign of the Sinhalese King Devānampiya Tissa.

4. Page ix. STATE-PLOUGH. It was the custom in old Lanka for the King to cut the first furrow of the State-Rice-fields, with a golden plough. King Tissa took this state-plough and ploughed the circle round the holy city.

5. Page x. ISURUMUNIYA-TEMPLE. The oldest Rock-Temple in Ceylon. It was hewn out of the solid rock by King Devanampiya-Tissa and it is now restored. Many Buddhist pilgrims visit this shrine and offer flowers before the statue of the Buddha in it.

6. Page x. THE RUANWELI-DAGABA was built by the famous Sinhalese King Duttu-Gemunu about 160 B.C. It was 270 feet high. The base was 2,000 feet in circumference. It is now being repaired. (See "*Stories from the History of Ceylon*" by M. Musaeus-Higgins.)

7. Page x. THE BODHI-TREE. Sangamitta, the sister of Mahinda and daughter of King Dharmasoka, brought a branch of the Bo-tree from Buddha-Gāya, to Ceylon (about 300 B C) It was planted at Anuradhapura during the reign of King Devanampiya Tissa and it stands there yet. It is considered to be the oldest historical tree in the world. Under the branches of this tree many pilgrims gather at all times specially on Full-moon-Days, which are the festival days of the Buddhists. It was under the old tree at Buddha-Gāya the Bodhisattva became a Buddha.

8. Page xi. See the book by the same author: "*Stories from the History of Ceylon.*"

9. Page xii. BORO-BUDHUR-TEMPLE. This Temple is in Jāva. It has recently been re-discovered. It is supposed to have been built about 850-900 A.D. when there must have been a Buddhist kingdom in Java At present there are no Buddhists in that island.

It is 111 feet high and built in five terraces round a hill. The inner walls of the terraces, to which one ascends by four staircases, have about 1600 *reliefs* on them. They illustrate, first the Buddhist hells, then some of the Jātakas, then the story of the life of Prince Siddhartha, who became the Buddha and lastly the Buddhist Heavens. On the top of this structure are 72 small dāgabas, each of them containing a statue of one of the Buddhas, which one can see through the stone trellis work. The summit is crowned by a larger Dāgaba, holding an immense unfinished statue, probably meant for the coming Buddha.

10. Page 197. TUSHITA-HEAVEN. The fourth Heaven of the Paradise of the Buddhists where the Bodhisattvas rest before they come back to earth. The Lord Maitreya Buddha is said to be there now.

11. Page 197. THE FIVE SIGNS ON EARTH OF A COMMING BUDDHA are,

(i) The right time.

(ii) The right country.

(iii) The right centre of the country (Jambudwipa India).

(iv) The right caste.

(v) The right mother.

12. Page 198. PRATYEKA BUDDHAS are Buddhas who do not preach the doctrine, but live retired.

13 Page 198. SAKYA. Solar Race.

14. Page 198. KAPILAVASTU. Western Bengal.

15. Page 198. ROHINI. Now called Kohana.

16. Page 202. BRAHMACHARIYA.—Ascetic member of a very strict Order of Monks.

17. Page 203. See Sir Edwin Arnold's description in book 1st of his "*Light of Asia.*"

18. Page 205. It is said that the seven signs which accompanied the birth of Prince Siddhartha were :—

(i) A beautiful light streamed over the world.
(ii) The blind received back their eyesight.
(iii) The crippled and the lame could walk.
(iv) The dumb could speak.
(v) The deaf could hear.
(vi) The drums sounded, without the drummers beating them.
(vii) The prisoners were released.

19. Page 206. ARGHA-SACRIFICE is brought to a Deva or a Brahmana. It consists of : Water, Milk, Kusa-Grass, Curd, Butter, Rice, Sesamum, and White Mustard.

20. Page 205 THE THIRTY-TWO SIGNS OF BUDDHAHOOD ARE :—

(i) A well formed head and forehead.
(ii) The hair is blue-black and shining. Each curl grows from left to right.
(iii) Forehead broad and straight.
(iv) Has a hair between the two eyebrows, turned to the right; it is as white as snow.
(v) The eyelashes are like those of a newly born calf in length and beauty.
(vi) Has shining blue-black eyes.
(vii) Has forty-teeth, all even.
(viii) The teeth are close together.
(ix) The teeth are pure white.
(x) His voice is like that of Māha-Brahmā.
(xi) He has exquisite taste.
(xii) His tongue is soft and long.
(xiii) His jaws are like those of a lion.

(xiv) Shoulders and arms are beautifully moulded.

(xv) Seven parts of the body are round and full.

(xvi) The space between the shoulders is well filled out.

(xvii) His skin has a golden colour.

(xviii) His arms are long, so that when he stands without bending, his hands can touch the knees.

(xix) The upper part of the body is like that of a lion.

(xx) His body is straight like that of Mahā-Brahmā.

(xxi) From each hair-sack a single hair grows.

(xxii) These hairs bend to the right at the top.

(xxiii) The organs of sex are hidden by nature.

(xxiv) The calves of his legs are full and round.

(xxv) His feet are like those of a deer in speed.

(xxvi) His fingers and toes are slender and of equal length.

(xxvii) His heels are long.

(xxviii) The instep of his foot is high.

(xxix) Feet and hands are delicate and long.

(xxx) A growth of epidermis covers the ends of the nails on fingers and toes, and thus prevents the collection of dirt.

(xxxi) His feet are flat and stand firmly.

(xxxii) Under the soles of his feet two shining wheels appear with a thousand spokes.

21. Page 211. THE SEVEN JEWELS ARE :—

(i) The jewel of the wheel, the symbol of earthly power, (later the wheel became the Swastika, the symbol of Buddhism.)

(ii) The white elephant.

(iii) The warrior steed.

(iv) The pearl.

(v) The woman.

(vi) The house-master.

(vii) The minister.

22. Page 212. TILAKE-SPOT.—The round mark on the forehead, between the eyes, which is only worn by women of high caste.

23. Page 232 MILK RICE.—In memory of this first meal of the Bodhisattva, after his long fast, it is yet the custom in Ceylon to have as first meal in a newly built house "milk-rice," (Kiri-bat) cooked by the mother or eldest daughter of the house.

24. Page 236. BUDDHA-GAYA.—Near Benares where the present Mahābodhi Temple stands. There stood the Bodhi-Tree (ficus religiosa) under which the Bodhisattva became the Buddha

25. Page 237. PATICCASAMMUPPADA.—The wheel of involution and evolution, whose spokes are the NIDANA. The twelve Nidanas form the chain of cansation which brings about the misery in the world. (See Oldenberg Buddha), Eng. tr. pp. 224—252.

26. Page 238. Quoted from "*The Gospel of Buddha*" by Paul Carus, page 33.

27. Page 242. THE FOUR NOBLE TRUTHS (from Col. Olcott's Buddhist Catechism.):—

(i) The miseries of evolutionary existence resulting in births and deaths, life after life.

(ii) The cause productive of misery, which is the selfish desire, ever renewed of satisfying one's self, without being able ever to secure the end.

(iii) The destruction of that desire, or the estranging one's self from it.

(iv) The means of obtaining this destruction of desire.

28. Page 243. THE NOBLE EIGHTFOLD PATH. The eight parts of this path are called añgas :—

(i) Right views (as to the law of cousation or Karma.)

(ii) Right Thought.

(iii) Right Speech.

(iv) Right Action.

(v) Right Means of Livelihood.

(vi) Right Exertion.

(vii) Right Concentration.

(viii) Right Meditation.

29. Page 243. THE THREE REFUGES or the three Guides are disclosed in the formula called Tisarana :—

" I follow the Buddha as my Guide.
I follow the Law as my Guide.
I follow the Order as my Guide."

30. Page 243. THE FIVE PRECEPTS (see note 2)

31. Page 244. BHIKKHUS.—Buddhist Monks or Priests.

32. Page 253. THE SALA-GROVE belonging to the King of the Mallas, called the Upavartana of Kusinagara, was by the river Hiranyavati, not far from Benares. It was in a beautiful garden, with many trees and flowering shrubs.

33. Page 254. THE FOUR DHYANAS ARE :—

(i) ' *Seclusion* in which you must force your mind from sensuality.

(ii) *Tranquillity* of mind, full of joy and gladness.

(iii) Taking delight in *Things Spiritual*.

(iv) The state of *Perfect Purity* and *Peace* in which the mind is above all gladness and grief."

" *Gospel of Buddha* " (Paul Carus.)

34. PAGE 254. PARI-NIRVANA. *Beyond* Nirvana, Nirvana extinction of lobha, dosa, moha, (lust, anger, delusion.) According to the Hinayâna it is defined as "extinction of illusion" (Paul Carus "*Gospel of Buddha.*")

Nirvana is the synonym of unselfishness, the entire surrender of selfhood to truth (Col. H. S. Olcott in his Buddhist Catechism.)

Sabbapāpassa akaranam.
Kusalassa upasampadā
Sacitto pariyodapanam
Etam Buddhanusāsanam.

To cease from every evil deed,
To bring good to perfection,
To purify one's thought,
This is the teaching of the Buddha.